TITHING:
The Biblically
Revealed Truth

TITHING:
The
Biblically
Revealed
Truth

Unraveling the biblical truth about tithing

B.C.O.T.
10%+

A.D.N.T
0%+

Earlington Guiste, Ph.D.
Evelyn Guiste, Ph.D.

XULON PRESS

Xulon Press
2301 Lucien Way #415
Maitland, FL 32751
407.339.4217
www.xulonpress.com

Printed in the United States of America.

ISBN-13: 9781545620670

Dedication

This book is dedicated to my family members and those very close friends who have embraced a mutual loyalty of friendship over the years. These include:

- the late Mr. & Mrs. Joseph & Josephine (Hayden) Guiste (my parents);

- Janet King, Lilia Stanford, Dalia Israel, and Judith Thomas, my loving sisters ;

- Evelyn Joseph Guiste, Ph.D. (wife) and Earlington E. H. Guiste (son) and my beautiful nieces and nephew.

My life-long friends, brothers- and sisters-in-Christ, who have remained in contact with me over the years:

- Alpha Josiah and his wife, the late Olive Josiah; and the late Alfred Richardson and family;

- Cordel and Ina Anthony, Fitzroy "King Fitz" Brathwaite, Leighton Daniel, Charlesworth Peters, Kathleen (Katie) Walter-Martin;

- Sylvester, Jean and Claude Charles (your generosity of '73 and friendship will always be remembered and cherished respectively and dearly).

Last but certainly not least are two dear friends and brothers-in-Christ, Dr. David Williams of Harvard University and Mr. Steven Thomas (M.S.) who have so willingly volunteered their time to read the manuscript and provide me with critical feedback. My sincere appreciation to both of you.

About the Authors

Earlington Guiste has truly developed a deep and abiding relationship with his Lord and Savior Jesus Christ. He sincerely loves his Savior and has dedicated his life to serving Him and His church. He was a teacher, principal, and former supervisor of a high school program. He is also the creator of TV and board games such as: SciTechMatics, The English Language Pyramid, DomiNations, Domination USA, Trinarow, Quadinrow etc. and is the leading author of this and The Unconventionality of Church Leadership.

He is married to Evelyn B. Guiste, Ph.D., co-author of this book, and they both have a son whose name is Earlington E. Guiste.

Earlington Guiste attended Caribbean Union College (now the University of the Southern Caribbean). Both authors attended and received their B.A. degrees from Oakwood College (now Oakwood University), Huntsville, Alabama; their M.A. degrees from Andrews University, Berrien Springs, Michigan; and their Ph.D. degrees from Michigan State University, East Lansing, Michigan (he, in College and University Administration with a cognate in the Sociology of Education and she, in Curriculum and Instruction and Computer Education).

He accepts invitations for his seven-part seminar presentations on church leadership and may be contacted at his email:

tripleegcompany@aol.com or phone # (781) 848-8084.

Table of Contents

Preface: Purpose & Method

The overall purpose of this book is to discover the biblical truth about tithing through a sagacious examination or analysis of most, if not all, textual tithing references in the Bible. And it is the **Bible** that will be utilized as the primary source and focus for this spiritually and intellectually enchanting journey since **it is the Christian's sole rule of faith and doctrine (Solo Scriptura).** Any other Christian literature consulted will be limited and considered secondary sources or lesser lights that lead to the greater light, the Word of God. And **"To the law and to the testimony: if they. . ."** the lesser lights, do not present information or analytically objective results or conclusions that are solely based on and are in congruence/harmony with the Word of God, or it/they **". . .speak not according to this word, it is because there is no light in them"** (Isaiah 8:20, KJV), they will be considered for exclusion from this text.

The study will also seek to understand both the direct and indirect instructions and or teachings on the tithing principle in both the O.T. and N.T. in order to discover if there is any link between them. And if there is no link, what circumstance(s) created the disconnect, rupture and or dissolution, and that which may be the motive for some modern

Christians to preach and or teach the relevance of the tithing principle in the New Dispensation.

It (the study) will also attempt to determine the impact, negative or positive, of Christ's death (on the cross) on the O.T. sacrificial system and its underpinning economic tithing principle in reference to the abrogation of the system and the suggested survival of the tithing component as the members of some Christians denominations believe, preach and teach. This will be done through a contextual examination of all New Testament passages of scripture used to support the tithing concept of the O.T. and let the Word reveal the truth about the disconnect or continuation of this idea into the Christian era.

Very limited extra-biblical sources and scholarly writings will be used or allowed to influence the objective conclusion drawn by the author. In other words, all scholarly Christian writings and their interpretations of those biblical tithing passages will be given very limited opportunity to influence the thinking and biblical conclusion of the author. The bible will be the significant source of inquiry, and if the English translations, in addition to the relatively limited application of biblical linguistics in the analysis for the writing of this text, cannot be trusted to reveal the essential tithing message of the Word, Christians are in serious trouble.

The assumption is that these translations are trustworthy and can be relied upon as written for a relatively complete comprehension of the Bible and the tithing principle. Therefore, I will allow the scripture to lead and I will follow, and its self-revealed conclusion on the current existence, relevance and or application of the tithing law/principle to the New Dispensation will be articulated.

If there is no specific or direct teaching in the N.T. on tithing, the study will endeavor to understand which particular economic method of giving has been introduced for the support of God's modern-day church and its ministries for the effectuation of the gospel commission in the New Dispensation. It is hoped that the biblically revealed truth about the validity and applicability, or the invalidation and inapplicability of the tithing principle in the Christian Dispensation will be discovered.

It is the biblical truth on tithing that is sought in spite of the economic inconvenience that it may cause some Christian denominations and independent churches.

Repetitions

T here are several repetitions made in this book particularly about the exclusive family selected for the priesthood and the functionary differences between the Levites and members of the Aaronic priesthood. These repetitions were consciously included in the text for reinforcement purposes and to remind readers of the distinct differences in the positions and roles of the Levites, the assistants to the priests, and the priests, and to compare the percentage of tithe allotted to the assistants (90%) versus that allotted to the priests (10%).

It is also to remind those who still believe in the misconception that the tithe was for the priests (incorrect) and therefore, if the modern-day pastors are considered to be a type of priests, the tithe is exclusively for them. Nothing can be further from the truth. If the Elders in Christian churches (the true biblical shepherd-servant leaders) are the assistants of the Pastors as is the current perception and practice, then they should be considered to be a type of Levites to whom 90% of the tithe should be allotted.

It is also to remind readers of some very significant information that was read and probably forgotten in a previous chapter or passage but has relevance for the clarity and or understanding of the new or current information. In other words, it is a way of reminding and helping the readers to connect previous information with that which is being currently read for greater comprehension. (Acronyms: O.T. means Old Testament; N.T. means New Testament; SS means Social Security).

Introduction and Pondered Questions

T here are numerous Christians who believe that the tithing concept is exclusively biblical. That it originated in the Bible as a
direct instruction given to Moses and Aaron by God for the Children
of Israel. Fortunately or unfortunately, the custom of paying a tenth
or a tithing system predates Israel's history and was not confined to
Semitic people but was very widespread and used by Indo-Germanic
peoples according to Brown 1978, p. 851.

In other words, the paying of tithes was not something unique
to the Jewish culture. According to extra-biblical literature, it was
employed in many places, sometimes as a political matter in reference
to a tax paid or imposed on a conquered nation by the conqueror. Or
it may have been a combination of both the sacred and secular. Brown
wrote that during Nebuchadnezzar's reign, a tithe from the land was
paid to the temple by all including the king while the Babylonian King
exacted a tithe from all imports. Persian satraps also demanded a tithe
of imports and Cyrus imposed on his soldiers a tithe to be paid to the
god Zeus. He also cited examples from Greece and Rome in which a

tithe tax on the land was occasionally dedicated to the gods (Brown, 1978, Vol. 3, p. 851).

There is also an apparently great divide in the Christian Church in reference to the validity of the tithing principle in the New Dispensation. Numerous Christians believe that the tithing precept is valid and quite a few believe that it has no relevance in the Christian era. And there are those who are unsure of its applicability in our modern economy. Many of those who believe in the transference of the tithe from the O.T. to the N.T. think that it should be calculated based on their gross income while others believe that it should be based on their net pay (or those who believe that the tithe should be based on and or deducted from their net pay). Then there are the business entrepreneurs who think that tithe should be paid after all business expenses, including taxes, are extracted/deducted from their business gross earnings, while many think that it should be based on the gross earnings of the business. The important questions for me at this juncture are: why are there so many variations in thinking on this subject matter? Is the biblical teaching on this concept not clear enough for a single perspective in interpretation? This is an idea that will be addressed later in this book.

At this point, it is necessary to arrive at a working definition of a tithe that will be utilized as the underpinning principle of this book. A tithe is a tenth according to Hebrew and Greek words. It is to take or give a tenth of something. This is assumed to be or mean a tenth part of anything or one in ten things, animals, or produce etc. If however, it is one in ten things that represents the ten percent, then this may not represent an equal ten percent if all ten things or products are not equal in reference to size, weight and quality. The general idea is to give that which appears to be a tenth and not to be legalistic about it especially in regards to produce in an agricultural economy.

What, however, is the underlying meaning of giving a tithe or ten percent of one's earning to the Lord? Many point to **Psalms 24:1** which reads: **"The earth is the Lord's and the fullness thereof; the world, and they that dwell therein"** and also in Psalms 50:10-12 in which David reiterated in more detail God's sovereign lordship and ownership over, not only the land, but also of the beasts of the field, the fowls of the air, the cattle and the entire world. What is the link, however, or how does a ten percent of one's earning from the land, or otherwise, demonstrate one's acknowledgement of and gratitude to God? Is gratitude a sincere attitude of gratefulness emanating from the heart and not a presentation of a certain amount of money and or produce? The giving or returning of money and or produce or products is probably just a symbol of one's gratitude, or it may just be an act or even a conviction that has no heart-felt basis, but one to satisfy friends, church members, church policy or to relieve one of the self-guilt felt as a result of the disparity of one's earning compared to others.

If the required portion (tithe) of money or products is unavailable due to one's inability to earn a living, how should such a person demonstrate his/her gratitude to God in light of the emphasis placed on tithe paying as a tangible symbol of one's gratitude? Should this individual be made to feel inadequate and appear to be ungrateful for the absence of the money-symbol gratitude? This becomes a problem when the symbols are given greater significance than that which

21

comes from the depth of one's soul, **"For thou desirest not sacrifice; else would I give it: thou delightest not in burnt offering. The sacrifices of God are a broken spirit: a broken and a contrite heart, O God, thou wilt not despise" (Psalms 51:16, 17).**

Before delving into the Old Testament to confirm the establishment of the sacrificial system by God, including the tithing component, let me expose you to some of the critical questions that I pondered over the years and did not discover the answers until relatively recently. It is the unanswered questions that motivated me to pursue some very serious studies of the Word of God and the writing of this book.

Pondered Questions

There is no doubt that the writing of this book is a culmination of a personal journey that has come to fruition through some in-depth study of the Word of God in order to discover biblically-based answers to many lingering questions that have gone unanswered for decades in my Christian experience. Especially those questions created by numerous ecclesiastical situations, in reference to stewardship presentations and sermons, that appeared to have been ineffective in linking the O.T. tithing principle with N.T. passages that apparently have little or nothing to do with tithing.

Some of the more serious and relevant questions that I have pondered and asked others over the years are:

If God is the Sovereign King and Owner of everything in the universe, and He is, why does anyone have to return to Him ten percent of his or her earned income in recognition of His ownership?

Why is a limitation placed on our giving, a tithe of ten percent, and is this sufficient to demonstrate the depth of our gratitude to Him for the priceless things He has done for us including the death of His Son on the cross for our eternal redemption?

Is our return of a tithe and offerings sufficient to curb our greed and selfishness? Does this type of giving have the power to transform our natural human inclinations? Don't rich people who are not Christians give to others and charities even more than what is given to the Lord by many Christians? Do motive and spiritual status count in God's sight?

If human beings were given dominion over His creation with a free will to choose, why are they not given the freedom to decide how much they should give back or give to the cause of God, and not to God because He does not need anything from us. That which He desires of us is expressed by David in Psalms 51:16, 17 (NIV),

> **"You do not delight in sacrifice, or I would bring it; you do not take pleasure in burnt offerings. The sacrifices of God are a broken spirit; a broken and contrite heart, O God, you will not despise."**

God desires our total beings as living sacrifices spiritually offered to Him in recognition of His love and benevolence in giving us life and a planet with the ability to sustain itself and life through its non-renewable and renewable resources. And when we give exceptionally serious consideration to the nature and cost of the most important thing He has done for us, His ultimate generosity in the giving of His

Son, Jesus Christ, as the living sacrificial Lamb of God on the cross for the redemption of the entire human race, how can anyone place a limit on the response of generic man to God? And I am here referring to the Christian's response in the New Dispensation.

Another significant idea that I considered was, when God required the Israelites to submit ten percent of their produce etc. for the Levites and Aaronic priests in addition to many different offerings, it is assumed that these were sufficient amounts that He knew were affordable for the givers and sustainable to the receivers in an agricultural economy with no government double and triple taxes, rent and mortgages, heating and light bills and the high cost of food, in a credit/monetary economy. Would it be a fair transference of the ten percent tithe and all the other offerings from that simple economic way of living to our present complex economy especially when one realizes the diverse wages of modern-day Christians with the application of the percentage across the board? Does one size fit all? Does a ten percent truly represent true proportionality as some think? Is the sacrificial nature of a poor man's 10% giving the same or similar to the 10% of a medium to rich person giving? And is there still a need today in the twenty-first century to strive for economic equality of means amongst God's people as did the early Christians?

All things being equal in reference to family size and needs with one family making $100,000.00 per year and the other at or below the poverty level making $20,000.00 or less per year after taxes for both, with the former returning $10,000.00 plus and the latter returning $2,000.00 plus in tithes etc. The former will have $90,000.00 to care for its needs etc. while the latter will have $18,000.00 to care for similar needs. This is by far a tremendous disparity that can never be considered proportional. God's children still need to help their brothers and sisters in need of economic assistance and otherwise.

There are also questions that emerged as a result of the method applied and emphasis placed on stewardship and tithing sermons. Many preachers and stewardship secretaries who preach and or make presentations in which they attempt to claim that money is not the emphasis, so they include such things as talents, time, possessions etc. but inevitably, they all end up emphasizing money. This is not to suggest that money is not of significance to the church in reference to its current structural operations and particularly to pay people and media for the gospel proclamation through all the world. However, there is a great emphasis in many Christian churches on money and even more so than on the weightier principles of the moral law.

A similar phenomenon is also seen on television. And that which is so disheartening or discouraging to see is the public fall of prominent TV preachers and the luxurious lifestyles lived by so many of them while the stench of poverty continues to permeate numerous homes of their parishioners and donors.

In those same sermon deliveries in which the goal of conversion/ salvation should be an inherent priority, what many experience is the guilt from the emphasis placed on not returning a faithful tithe and the status of being a thief or stealing from God, without any regard for where each person is in his/her spiritual experience with Jesus. Should the objective of preaching and other related presentations and teachings be that of making their hearers guilty when they enter the body of Christ or church to worship Him? Or should the gentle voices of the shepherds be applied in leading people to a deeper spiritual experience with the Master from where all good things should flow?

Too many people walk out the church and do not return as a result of the implied or guilt-ridden emphasis in preaching on tithing. And to add insult to injury, there are those prominent preachers and stewardship personnel who would say in a heart beat that all who question the concept of tithing or have any doubt etc. is reflected on the church books. This means that a review of the treasurer's books will reveal that those with questions are those who do not pay tithe. This is not necessarily so. There may be a multiplicity of reasons why they have questions, one of which is that too many Christians do not earn sufficient income to adequately provide for their families which in essence creates a significant guilt in the minds of those people, something which is compounded when they enter God's church to worship and another layer of psychological guilt is laid on without any real concern for the financial circumstances of these people. Where is the true love?

In addition to the immediate above, there are times in the stewardship or tithing sermon deliveries that one is able to sense and even "slice" the thick fog of self-interest in those presentations. It does appear that because the preachers' salaries are based on the collected tithe, there is that extra energy exerted to impose and solidify in the minds of the hearers the grave consequences of not returning a faithful tithe. There is that sense that when pressure is exerted, guilt will be produced and compliance will follow, and all will be well for the beneficiaries and the guilt-ridden members also.

Two of the most significant questions that have always remained with me are the following: 1. Why is there no direct teaching on tithing in the New Testament subsequent to the death of Christ on the cross? And, 2. If this is such a critical aspect of the Christian's spiritual experience, then why is it that Jesus (after His death), Paul, John, Matthew, Peter, Luke nor any other New Testament writer ever wrote any direct statement and or teaching on returning a faithful tithe and offering to God as was emphatically taught in the Old Testament?

Jesus appeared to have made some cursory remarks about tithing in Matthew 23:23, but this was prior to His death on the cross. And does His remark(s) indicate the valid transference of the tithing system to the New Dispensation? Was Paul also attempting to indicate the same in the book of Hebrews where he referred to Abraham paying tithes to Melchizedek and the Israelites paying tithes to the Levites? These will be explored in this book.

Another not-so-important question is, why is it that the Christian Church does not take a firmer stand against those members who do not comply with the tithing principle, if it is still applicable, and if their non-compliance is considered a contravention of the eight commandment which is, "Thou shalt not steal."? Some churches that believe in the existence or the applicability of the tithing law in the New Dispensation will deny non-tithe payers any opportunity to function in church "offices" and use their gifts in the service of God. This approach will not convince those members to return a faithful tithe if they do not believe in the validity of tithe paying in the Christian era. In addition, the church will forfeit the utilization of those members' gifts in the building up of the saints.

How about those members who work in the medical and related professions, and are on their jobs during the specified worship day of the week? They may pay a faithful tithe but are they not breaking the fourth commandment and are just as guilty or even more so, due to the moral nature of the commandment violation, than those who do not believe in tithe paying which is not a part of the Ten Commandments or God's moral law? You decide.

When the Sabbath of the fourth commandment (established by God through His resting on it and His proclamations of it as being blessed and made holy in Gen. 2:3) and the other nine were articulated on/in stone with the finger of God, there were no exceptions made in them for medical personnel. Jesus is the One who introduced the emergency component as an exception on the Sabbath day to deal with the saving of lives etc. and then returning to Sabbath keeping subsequent to the emergency (O.T. example is David eating the showbread to which he was not entitled but necessary to save his and his fighting men, etc.). But with the institutionalization of emergencies – hospitals and clinics etc. – requiring Christians to violate the fourth commandment on a regular basis, it appears that the emergency component has been extracted from the nature of Christ's intention of emergency. And if this is truly a serious Sabbath keeping violation, would the tithe paid from those hours of work be acceptable to God?

Is there any objective rationale for this type of service which seems to contravene Sabbath keeping? The one that I have heard is that the sick must be cared for even on the Sabbath Day. But is this a sound theological justification for that violation? There may be a strong biblical argument that can be made for this apparent contravention and this, the nature of the work and Christ's conclusion in reference to serving others in that *"... Inasmuch as ye have done it unto one of the least of these my brethren, ye have done it unto me"* (Mat. 25:40, KJV). Or how about the priestly function in the Temple on the Sabbath Day that was considered to be a violation but due to the sacred nature of their work, it was not held against them. Can this claim be made by anyone in modernity? Whatever we do as individuals in reference to this matter, consistently consult in a persevering manner with Jesus and listen closely to the still small voice of the Holy Spirit for the answer.

In addition, those churches that do not disassociate or revoke the membership of non-tithe paying members appear to be disingenuous in not holding them accountable to the high ideals of the Christian faith. This may be a weak analogy, but if the IRS knew that there were citizens who were not paying taxes, there would be an immediate crack down on those people. So why do these churches tolerate those none tithe-paying members if they are contravening such a significant principle of the Christian faith? It is understandable that the church does not possess the legal power to enforce the tithing law, if applicable, as governments do in enforcing their laws, but it must take a principled stand through any practical means of encouragement, if the tithing law is applicable in the Christian era, to deal with known violations of biblical principles or they will lose their spiritual appeal over time if left solely to individually voluntary compliance.

Another question arises out of the link that is made between tithing and the successful proclamation of the gospel message. The implication is that the gospel dissemination is enabled only through tithing that is used to compensate full-time gospel workers and or preachers. This linkage is said to be responsible for the magnificent growth of the Christian Church and if broken, will result in massive church growth reduction. My question is, where is the scriptural evidence? And does this idea undermine the power of the Holy Spirit to work with individuals to share the gospel on a smaller scale and with a more effective method/approach?

Other questions in reference to the tithing and gospel proclamation link are: Why is it that the Jehovah Witnesses and the Mormon Church have achieved such exponential growth and they do not believe in the tithing principle and have no paid clergy? Why is it that the Roman Catholic Church experienced such global growth over hundreds of years with no tithing system in place and no paid clergy? Is there any valid theological reason for the dismissal of the tithing principle as being an irrelevant biblical teaching in the Christian era? It appears that they employed the early Christian method of freewill giving and other imposed methods of giving that supplied sufficient funds for their effective operations. This is a challenge for some M.A. or doctoral students to pursue an objective investigation into this phenomenon.

The most important circumstance that I refer to as the "straw that broke the camel's back" and precipitated this personal journey of research and the writing of this book, was based on my encounter with an untrained and unqualified "pastor" who was very obsessed with the O.T. tithing law. He invited an evangelist to conduct a three-week evangelistic crusade in 2007 in the State of Massachusetts and that which was so astonishing was the timing and positioning of a sermon on tithing early in the second week which seemed so inappropriate. Even before he had preached about the significance of Christ's exemplary life, death and or resurrection, he delivered a sermon on tithing. The links he made and the inferences he drew between the O.T. tithing principle and the N.T. passages had no contextual bearing or relevance to tithes, and it was very unbearable to hear. That which was even more disturbing, however, were the few "amens" that indicated some listeners' impulsive or spontaneous reaction, and or their convictions on what they were taught and or heard.

This situation was further compounded by a very distinguished scholar on Stewardship who, during a weekend of stewardship presentations, provided an answer to a member's question about the setting aside of one's tithes and offerings on the first day of the week in reference to the passage in 1Cor. 16:2. His response was a confirmation that it should be done until he was challenged by the author who mentioned that the textual context had no relevance to tithing. He responded by saying that it had to do with the tithing principle. The answer provided, as far as the author was concerned, was incorrect and or irrelevant. The passage has more to do with the broader stewardship principle and not with the tithing principle.

One of the exceptionally surprising and very disturbing circumstances that propelled me to conduct a serious investigation into the tithing issue occurred several years ago, in 2003. I was pondering many of the above questions and remembered a friend of mine who, with numerous years of experience in both education and pastoral ministry, was in a position to provide some of the answers I was seeking. He was serving in an office/ministry that was highly related to the subject matter and was preaching, and probably teaching (seminars) about stewardship which included sermons on tithing and offerings etc. His studies, position and professional experiences should have equipped him with the knowledge and wisdom to provide some biblically objective answers to, if not all, many of the above-mentioned questions.

So after serious consideration, I access the organizational website and sent him an email with a few questions on tithing with the expectation of receiving some sound biblically-based objective answers that would have assisted me in making the right decision(s). Instead, I received an unexpectedly very personal response which I will exclude from this book. However, the following was my response that, by deduction, will provide the essence of his response.

June 1, 2003. Thank you for responding to my response to your article on Stewardship. I tried to send you a response through e-mail but there was a rejection for some unknown reason. My original intention for responding to your article was to initiate an intellectually objective dialogue or exchange of stewardship ideas through questions and answers or responses due to my keen interest in the area (motivated by a year of Stewardship studies with Pastor Harold Lee at CUC and performing at the highest level) and hopefully with the expected outcome being that of a clearer understanding of the application of stewardship principles and a deeper spiritual experience. However, the tone and content of your response were very perplexing for the following reasons:

1. The level of your discomfort in discussing or exchanging the above-mentioned ideas with {members of a particular denomination} (you made an exception for new members and non-...). I am totally convinced that anyone who has the intelligence to believe and take a religious, philosophical or any other position on any issue and publishes it, should be prepared to defend it. We, Christians, should be ready to give an account of that which we believe to all people.

2. Your statement about my longevity in the church by referencing my birth in, growing up in, seminary education in, and your wondering about the reasons for my questions being the "...result of [my] ...spiritual journey or an evolution in [my] ... theological life." And

3. Your preference in discussing such matters/issues with me if I was still a "...fellow worker, being paid from the same tithe that [I am] ... now questioning its use" and that I did not raise such issues with you during my employment with the {organization}, so "...why do so now?"

Since I read these statements and final question, I have been struggling to determine their place and relevance in an intellectually issue-oriented dialogue. Being born in, or having grown up in the church; or receiving a seminary education should not limit my cognitive ability to think "party line" and cease the questioning of the alignment of the church's policies, structure and actions with biblical principles. If church members are afraid to question church decisions and other related matters surrounding or sanctioned by the beneficiaries of the current system, how will we, as a church, grow and develop (change for the better) to maturity in Christ and ascertain a more egalitarian church. As a rock-solid . . ., I am very concerned about how often we question or turn the probing light on other denominations or religions but find it so excruciatingly painful to shine it on ourselves for fear of discovering our shortcomings. We may have a "perfect" gospel, but we are not a perfect people. Human nature has not changed over the last six thousand years and this applies to {. . .} also. There are still sheep and goats in the church, imbedded in both the artificial divisions of laity and clergy.

This is the reason why we need more Martin Luthers in our church; people who are willing and ready to elevate themselves above the parochial politics of the church and dare risk everything for the truth and our Redeemer. I attended a . . . Elders Training Seminar conducted by the . . . Church pastor and a couple of his elders. In talking about the significance of good leadership to organizations, he mentioned about what normally happens when organizations (including sport teams) are performing poorly. He emphatically said that the leaders are the ones who are fired, not the employees or players. I eventually asked him what should happen in the . . . Conference in light of the financial difficulties and he pretended as though he was Jesus standing in the presence of Pilate, he said not a word. By the way, Pastor . . . was present. Was his none response wisdom or job protection? My wife's sister lost her job when she acted upon the Sabbath truth for Jesus, and numerous others have suffered the same fate. Then what do they find in the church? Leaders who are afraid to stand up for the truth for fear of {losing} their jobs. Where is their faith in Christ to provide another job in the event they are fired for their stand?

You also mentioned that I never raised the tithing issue with you when I was paid from the tithe during my employment with the conference. My response is that if I was, it was not my decision but that of the conference administration (the leaders). They will be held accountable for their misappropriations, and so will we if we are cognizant of this spiritually objectionable situation and remain silent as an indication of our condonation or support of such an action. In addition, when I was a conference worker, you were not the Stewardship Director with a publicly posted internet article on Stewardship, and therefore, no reason to have raised such an issue with you. Remember, the questions were raised as a result of the (your) published article.

What I am more concerned about is the implication of your statement which seems to suggest that as an employee, I was more than willing to compromise my principle. I have always questioned a number of church-related decisions and that may be partly respon-sible for my severance from the church as an employee. There are too many church leaders who despise the questioning of any decision etc. made by them in the context of the church.

In reference to the financial difficulties of the . . . Conference, you mentioned the reason being that of past mismanagement and limited that to the overemployment of workers. Then you concluded that "Anything else you hear is not the truth." I will broaden mismanage-ment to include the written or unwritten policy of the conference that sanctioned the keeping of the tithe by several church missions that far exceeded a million dollars for the purchase of church buildings. Don't you think that the result of such a policy would contribute in a significant way to a greater budget deficit and be considered a gross contravention of the biblical tithing principle? Is there any {biblical} precedence for such an application of the tithe? Or are we, as a church, given divine authority to interpret and apply the tithing principle in a broader light and with greater flexibility? You may or may not respond to these questions.

I am convinced that in this world, we will continue to have many more questions than answers, but I am assured that God has provided for us sufficient information in His word for our salvation. Therefore, when I am asked a question for which I do not have an answer, I can confidently and honestly say, I do not know.

It is my sincere hope that this dialogue can continue without prejudice. God bless and give our regards to . . . . .

It was then that I, the author, decided to look deeper into the issue, **from a biblical perspective**, although I had completed a six-year theology program in which was included a two-quarter study of Stewardship under the tutelage of the most distinguished lecturer in this field, Dr. Harold Lee. The biblical truth that I discovered in this journey is of great interest and enlightenment to me, and I hope to all those who will read this book.

Let us turn our attention to the O.T. and examine those passages of scripture that should provide critical information on what God communicated to Moses and Aaron in reference to the introduction and establishment of the sacrificial institution. That is, how He selected several components: the sanctuary, its structure and contents;

sacrifices; tithe and offerings; and all the other ceremonial laws for the effective and efficient governance and or operation of the system. These components were well integrated into an inseparable institution for the immediate and daily benefit of His children, and as a medium that pointed them to the future prophetic fulfillment of the sacrificial Lamb of God, Jesus Christ, who would come to earth in the form of a man and be sacrificed/slain once and for all times to redeem the human family from eternal destruction.

Chapter I

Tithing In the Old Testament

Abram's (Abraham's) Tenth

The first passage of scripture that seems to have some relevance to tithing, a tenth or tithe paying, is found in **Genesis 14:20 and it reads: ". . . blessed be this most high God, which hath delivered thine enemies into thy hand. And he gave him tithes of all."**

Without going into great details, it is needful to understand the context of this tithe presentation and the reason(s) for it, including Abram's (Abraham) war involvement. Abram and his nephew, Lot, had entered Canaan and due to the growth of both families and their owned animals/possessions, there was an amicable division and or separation. Lot chose to live, according to Genesis 13:12, 13, ". . .in the **cities of the plain, and pitched his tent toward Sodom. But the men of Sodom were wicked and sinners before the Lord exceedingly,"** while Abram dwelt in the plain of Mamre in Hebron.

Unfortunately, the kings of several nations went to war, including the kings of Sodom and Gomorrah, and they lost everything as a result of their defeat. Even Lot, his family members and possessions were captured, and taken away. Abram was informed of his nephew's capture, and he and his fighting men pursued the kings, defeated them and saved Lot and his family members, and all his goods. On their way home, the king and priest of Salem whose name was Melchizedek **". . .brought forth bread and wine: and he was the priest of the most high God" (Genesis 14:18, 20).** And he blessed Abram who **". . . gave him tithes of all."**

Melchizedek, though introduced here for the first time in the Bible, appears to be a man of great distinction. He was both the king and priest of Salem (Jerusalem) but what kind of priest was he? Was he a priest who believed in the true God, the One in whom Abram believed? Based on the "fact" that Abram gave him tithes appears to be sufficient grounds/evidence to assume that he was. However, it is very difficult to comprehend how such a king-priest existed amongst the so-called wicked Canaanites and Amorites in Abram's time, but we can only assume that God always has His representatives in every era and amongst all peoples.

Does the information of Abram paying tithes to Melchizedek provide all the necessary data needed to draw the conclusion that this act ". . .proves that Abram was well acquainted with the sacred institution of tithe paying"? (ABC, Vol.1, p. 309). There is the need to provide some historically documentary or scriptural evidence to support this idea or conclusion. Scripture reveals that Abram built several altars to the Lord; that he even built one on which he was about to offer his son as a sacrifice to God which appears to be a continuation of the sacrificial system that goes all the way back to Cain and Abel, the latter of whose offering God respected but frowned on that of Cain which led to Abel's death. But there is no scriptural evidence to support the idea of a "sacred institution of tithe paying" prior to the action of Abram. In addition, there is nothing else written about the distinguished king-priest until David mentioned his name in Psalms 110:4 and Paul referred to him in the book of Hebrews 5, 6, and 7.

What was it that prompted Abram to give a tithe of the spoil of war when there is no apparent scriptural precedence for it? Abram may have been justified in going to war to reclaim his nephew, family and possessions, but should this be a moral/ethical example for Christians to follow and present a tenth of the spoils to priests, pastors or the church? Would such a tithe be considered an appropriate deduction from the gains of one's questionable labor based on the Old Testament tithing principle? Or was this encounter a **spiritual aberration** designed to set the stage as a type of priest with whose order Christ's priesthood would be associated and compared at a future time? And should it be considered as a forerunner of the tithing system God intended to institute in Israel? Whatever the intent, one thing is apparent and that is, there was no written law demanding this action by Abram and there is no scriptural reason presented as to why he gave the tithes.

There is need to question the correct amount of tithe paid by Abram from the (or is it a gesture of scriptural symbolism) spoil due to what is written later in verse 21 in which the king of Sodom requested his people from Abram while permitting him to keep the goods. But in verse 23 and 24, Abram pledged not to keep anything that was the king's, save only that which the *". . .young men have eaten, and the portion of the men which went with me, Aner, Eshcal and Mamre,* *let them take their portion."* Of what did he pay tithe? Did he capture spoils from the other enemy kings of Sodom and Gomorrah and paid tithe from that spoil? This seems to be the implication and not tithing on the whole spoil.

Does it mean as is suggested or stated in the ABC that Abram's action of paying tithe *". . .shows clearly that this institution was* *not a later, temporary expedient to provide for the sacrificial ser-* *vices, but that it was a divinely instituted practice from earliest* *times"* (ABC, vol. 1, p. 309). If this statement is correct, then one can legitimately ask, at what point in time was this practice instituted or established? To whom was the tithe paid and for what purpose in light of the fact that all priestly functions were conducted by the heads of households or the family patriarchs as was mentioned previously. It is very significant to provide some type of biblical or extra biblical documentary evidence to corroborate such an idea or suggestion.

If this was/is such a critically permanent institution established by God for all times and transcends all cultures; and if this was so signifi-cant to the redemption of the human family, why is there no scriptural record of this as an organized practice for God's people prior to its institution in post-Egyptian Israel? Even though it is understood that every detail of God's plans is not recorded in scripture, there is no evidence from the children of Adam and Eve, and all the generations following to Enoch, Methusalah, Noah on down to Abram's father, that there was such institution. In other words, the patriarchs built their own altars and offered sacrifices without directing their actions to a select priesthood. Scriptural evidence of this is found in Genesis

8:20 (Noah's); Genesis 12:6; 13:18; 22:9 (Abraham's); Genesis 26:25 (Isaac's); Genesis 33:20; 35:1-7 (Jacob's); and Exodus 17:15 (Moses'). This would have been too important an institution to have been omitted from scripture. It appears, however, that the said statement (the early institution of tithing) is a modern-day rationalization for the continued implementation of a reliable and dependable financial source with a proven record to generate sufficient funds for the operations of the church in light of its apparent abrogation at the cross. Or is it that the church has not discovered a better economic system to meet its financial needs?

It seems, to this point in time, that one is able to make the conclusive argument that there is insufficient evidentiary documentation to substantiate the idea of an institution of the tithing law prior to and independent of the institutionalized sacrificial system. Even if there was such a practice, would that have provided the condition of immunity from obsolescence when Christ died on the cross?

A similar argument can be articulated for the animal sacrifice as a sin offering that was instituted immediately after the Fall of man as was evidenced in the presentation of Abel's sin offering. Did its establishment prior to and independent of the institutionalized sacrificial system provide a similar condition to exclude it from abrogation at the cross? One may rationalize, if needed to justify the implementation of an aspect of the annulled sacrificial system, that such a component was instituted prior to and independent of, therefore, the death of Christ would have no effect on it and its implementation in the New Dispensation.

A similar justifiable argument can also be made about the priesthood since Abram paid tithe to the king-priest, Melchizedek. His priesthood was established prior to the sacrificial institution and independent of it, therefore, it warranted exclusion at the death of Christ. One thing is very clear and that is, God brought all the necessary components together, including the ceremonial laws, for the institutionalization of the sacrificial worship services and if any part of such a system survived the cross, biblical evidence should be put forward without any extrapolation.

Jacob and His Tenth

Unfortunately, nothing else is revealed in scripture about Abram or any other tithe paying to any other priest until we read about Jacob in Genesis 28:22. Jacob had deceived his father to receive the blessing of the birth right due to Esau, the first born, and was admonished to leave home in order to avoid the wrath of Esau's anger following its discovery. He survived the night in the wilderness, received a dream from God and a reiteration of the Abrahamic covenant, and upon awakening from his sleep in fear, he vowed that if God kept him safe and provided for him, ***"So that I come again to my father's house in peace; then shall the Lord be my God: And this stone, which I have set for a pillar, shall be God's house: and of all that thou shalt give me I will surely give the tenth unto thee"*** (Genesis 28:21, 22).

The difficulty with this passage is not an absence of a tithe paying precedence, but to whom did he pay the tenth if he did and for what purpose was it used? Were there Levitical ancestors or assistants to the priests appointed by God in his time to receive tithes? If there was no priest, how did he dispense with the tenth as pledged. Was he allowed to perform some spiritual or religious ritual, or act of worship, present it to God and consume it in God's presence as an offering to Him? The record is lacking this information but a pledge/vow of this nature/magnitude from a man who was that close to the true God, can only be assumed to have been paid by Jacob.

O.T. Sacrificial System Established, Exodus 25
(Sanctuary, Priesthood and Levitical Assistants Introduced).

In Exodus 25:8, the process of introducing the institution of the sacrificial system to the Children of Israel who were in Egypt for four hundred and thirty years (many generations in a so-called heathen land) commences with: *"And let them make me a sanctuary; that I may dwell among them."* Then instructions in reference to the structure of the sanctuary were given, and in chapter 28, instruction was given to take Aaron, Moses' brother and his four sons, to set them apart to *". . .minister unto me in the priest's office."* In addition, all specifications regarding the type of clothing they were to wear in their ministry were also provided.

This said instruction was given directly to Aaron in reference to his and his sons' priestly responsibilities as follows:

> *"Thou and thy sons and thy father's house with thee*
> *shall Bear the iniquity of the sanctuary: and thou*
> *and thy sons with thee shall bear the iniquity of your*

priesthood" (Numbers 18:1, KJV), and ". . .minister before the tabernacle of witness" (vs. 2). "And ye shall keep charge of the sanctuary, and the charge of the altar" (vs. 5). "Therefore thou and thy sons with thee shall keep your priest's office for every thing of the altar, and within the vail; and ye shall serve: I have given your priest's office unto you as a service of gift: and the stranger of that cometh nigh shall be put to death" (vs. 7).

Then instructions were provided regarding those who would serve or assist the priests in certain sanctuary functions such as assembling and dismantling the portable sanctuary/tent when they traveled from place to place, in conjunction with the caring for it in reference to cleaning etc. and other administrative duties for the orderly and timely operations of the worship services. These non-priestly brethren (the tribe of Levi of which Aaron, his sons and his father's sons, were a part) were selected to assist the priests (Numbers 1:49-51; 3:6, 7). In other words, they were to: *". . . keep charge of the tabernacle of the congregation, for all the service of the tabernacle"* (Numbers (18:4) or *". . .to do the service of the tabernacle of the congregation" (vs. 6).*

God selected the entire tribe of Levi *". . .from among the children of Israel instead of all the firstborn that openeth the matrix among the children of Israel: therefore the Levites shall be mine"* (Numbers 3:12), and set them apart specifically to serve in the sanctuary services. But why did He select this tribe for such important roles in Israel? The reason for the selection of this tribe, Levi, appears to be inherent in the text as a substitute for the *"first born that openeth the matrix."* Based, however, on Exodus 19:4-6, it seems that God's original intention was for the whole of Israel to become a nation of priests (Deut. 7:6; 14:2; 26:18) but He ended up with the Levites and the selective family of Aaron. It is assumed by some that Israel in general did not live up to God's will but the Levites did, and they were chosen for this special role. Whether this is the case or not, the biblical record indicates very clearly that their selection was God's choice and that does it for me.

And out of this tribe, He appointed a small number, the house of Aaron, his father's, and his sons to hold the office of the priesthood and to perform certain priestly functions within the veils of the sanctuary. These people were to devote their entire lives to the said appointed offices/roles. They were not permitted to do any other work in Israel nor could they have any inheritance. Therefore, God arranged the economic means (the tithing system) to support the entire tribe in an agrarian society.

Tithe and Offerings Introduced

All the offerings, including the sacrificial ones (the fat to be burned on the altar), were all allotted/given to the Aaronic priests in addition to a tenth of the tithe from all Israel. The tithe was given by God to the tribe of Levi as their inheritance and as a payment for their service in the tabernacle (Numbers 18:21, 31). When the same tribe of Levi collected the tithe from all Israel, they in turn were to *". . .offer up an heave offering of it for the Lord, even a tenth part of the tithe"*

(Numbers 18:26) ". . .and ye shall give thereof the Lord's heave offering to Aaron the priest" (vs. 28).

Several things are critically significant at this juncture and they are as follows:

1. A system of tithe and offerings was instituted (or reinstituted as some think) for the economic support of the Levites, including the priests, as a reward for the work they performed in the tabernacle. According to Leviticus 27:30, the tithe of everything in Israel belonged to God and was considered to be holy which fundamentally means that they were set aside for holy purposes or to reward those who served in the tabernacle.

2. The tithe was collected and used for the sole purpose of **rewarding** or **paying those who rendered services**, the Levites and Aaronic priests, **in the sanctuary**. It, the tithe, was dedicated to God (it was His), and He in turn declared it holy and gave it to the Levites (the priests received only ten percent of it) who were exclusively selected by God to serve as assistants to the priests in their performance of specific functions in the sanctuary. They were not permitted to engage in any other line of work and had no inheritance in Israel.

3. The tithe was not for the priests. They received only a tenth or ten percent (10%) of the tithe. The other ninety percent (90%) of it went to the non-priests, the Levites, as compensation for their work in the sanctuary. In other words, the Levites collected the tithe from the people and they in turn were expected to tithe the tithe and give that portion to the priests (Numbers 18:26, 28; Nehemiah 10:37, 38).

It should be noted here that the priests did not collect the tithe; they only received a tenth of all the Levites collected. So that ninety percent went to those who worked in the sanctuary in non-priestly roles. The priests were supported only by the tenth of the tithe in conjunction with the offerings brought to the sanctuary by the people.

4. The priesthood was reserved exclusively for one family, that of Aaron and his father's and their sons. The Levites, of whom Aaron and his father had genealogical ties, could not seek the office of the priesthood. This was strictly a family affair; a family chosen by God to perform certain sacred responsibilities on behalf of the people with God. No person from any other tribe could assume such a function or role. A good example or one taking action as a priest was **KORAH** (Numbers 16:1-35) and the consequence was grave – death.

The above were very restrictive regulations included in a system that God institutionalized and became known as the sacrificial system. The following components were included and these became interdependently integrated into this system. These are:

1. The sanctuary with its contents, without going into great details, was a physical structure that was 150 feet long and 75 feet wide, and comprised of three compartments that included the Most Holy Place where the presence of God resided and the only location where the High Priest alone was allowed to enter; the Holy Place where the priests administered the

sacrificial blood and incense; and the Outer Court where the people brought their sin offerings or animal sacrifices to be killed and offered. This was the fundamental structure of the O.T. church and the differences between it and the N.T. church will be dealt with in chapter 3.

It should be noted here, however, that the offering of the animal sin sacrifices administered through the mediatorial role of the priests was the central focus of the system. The entire sanctuary structure and most of the furnishings were specifically designed for the blood sacrifices and the remission of the individual and collective sins of Israel during the worship services which is very different to that of the church in the new dispensation; **2.** the priesthood, in spite of its independent existence prior to the time of Abram; **3.** the Levitical helpers; **4.** the tithe and offerings of all types, in spite of their suggested independent existence prior to their inclusion in this institution; and **5.** the ceremonial laws that were introduced for the proper guidance and operation of the entire system. All these were brought together under one very well integrated institutional umbrella.

This means that all these parts were so well integrated, interrelated, intertwined and interdependent that the separation of any one would result in the disintegration of the whole system. This integrative interrelationship was clearly demonstrated when the Children of Israel refused to give tithe and offerings, a situation that forced the Levites and priests to neglect the sanctuary and its services in order to work the land for a living (Nehemiah 13:10, 11). If the priesthood was taken away, or the Levitical helpers, or the sanctuary, or the sacrifices, the system would not be able to function as God intended it.

The question of great interest here is what occurred when the system was made null and void at the death of Christ on the cross? Did a part or parts of it survive and is or are eligible for integration into the new Christian era? This is central to the essence of this book.

The implication of the priesthood, as mentioned earlier, is that even though a person was a member of the Levi tribe, he had no tribal right to the priesthood. It was relegated to or reserved only for Aaron's and his father's family and following generations. If a male in Israel had no genealogical connection to the family of Aaron, he had no right to and was forbidden from pursuing the priestly office regardless of his priestly ambitions, and or any expressed inner calling to the office he may have experienced and verbally expressed. God's call and selection were extended only to the members of a specific family in spite of how corrupt the whole priesthood eventually became almost from the beginning and all through the many generations.

This idea of non-priests collecting tithe, and offering a tithe or tenth part of it to the priests is supported in the Adventist Bible Commentary, Vol. 1, P. 885 which states that "...of all that came to their hand the Levites were to make their offering to the priests." On the other hand, it is stated that the "...priests were devoted to God (Deut. 10:9). On their part, the people were to manifest a spirit of generosity toward their brethren the priests." Why? Because the priests lived from God's altar and were fed at God's altar (ABC Vol. 1 p. 884).

The statement seems to suggest that the people could be generous to the priests but not to the Levites who did the hard work. This is understood in light of the fact that the portion of the tithe kept by the Levites was an established ninety percent, with the priests receiving only ten percent of it. In addition, the priests received all the offerings that were excluded from a numerical percentage and the amount contributed was left to the discretion of the givers for the most part even though first fruits and other things were mentioned. Therefore, they could be encouraged to give generously or beyond that which they were mandated to give.

On the other hand, one begins to wonder why would the people be encouraged to discriminate in their giving by being generous to the priests and not to the Levites? Working at the altar does not give one any special right to demand, request or expect special favors from those whom they were appointed to serve. Any generosity should be equitably shared amongst all workers in God's Old Testament church. It is also hoped that this statement was not articulated to reinforce in the minds of Christians their obligation to be generous to pastors as is demonstrated in so many churches and expected by so many of the clergy who work for salaries that exceed, in general, the average earned salary of numerous Protestant Christians. The reverse is what should be encouraged in this modern age.

What are the implications, however, for ministry and or pastoral ministry in modernity? Let us assume for now that the institution of the tithing system has relevance for today, in the year 2017. If it does, why is the distribution structure not the same or similar to the original one? Does God have to call directly those who work full-time in His church today, and are they entitled to one-tenth of the tithe to be divided among them? And to what are those who provide other services in the church entitled? Does it still mean that only descendants of Aaron's and his father's family can be "priests?" And how about the descendants of the tribe of Levi? Is any family member acceptable to God to function in the church of the New Dispensation? And if the rule of a specific family and its descendants only can fill the office of the priesthood, did the rule die with the abrogation of the sacrificial system? And if we are all priests since Christ died on the cross, why do some believe that they are entitled to the tithe and no one else? And if the tithe is designed for the Levites and priests who were selected by God and there is no genealogical records to determine who is connected to this family, are modern Christians still obligated to give tithe to those who are not a part of the aforementioned tribe and family?

According to God's plan as was instituted in the book of Numbers, the tithe was designed for those who worked in the sanctuary—the Levites who were non-priests. In addition, the same Levites or workers were the ones who collected the tithes, tithe it and gave a tenth to the priests as their portion or reward. They (the priests) had no obligation to pay tithe to anyone in Israel. The "buck" stopped with them. So why is it that the modern-day pastors/ministers/priests who are considered by many to be a type of priest pay tithe of their salaries for the services they render in the church? Are they a type of priest or a type of Levite who paid tithe to the priests? The comparison serves only to recreate that socio-religious division that existed between God's people in the O.T. and something for which Christ died to destroy. It also serves as a contradiction of the all-believer priesthood principle.

In the modern church or Christian era, the "priests" or pastors are the ones who control the tithe and how it is spent, and those who work hard in the "sanctuary" or church such as the elders, deacons, youth leaders and other officers etc. are excluded from any reward or payment for their work or contribution in the church. Why are the tithes used to reward people who do not directly perform any local church-related duties such as certain officials as presidents, secretaries, security guards, custodians and musicians and a host of others while those who directly perform very important roles in the church are expected to volunteer their time and told that their reward is in heaven? Why is it that the ministers/pastors are generally the only ones who are rewarded for their work in the local "sanctuary" or church? Why should a specific group and small minority of God's people who play a minor role in gospel dissemination be paid while the vast number of people who hit the pavement going door to door with the gospel message are denied any share of the tithe? Why must some people be rewarded here on earth for their labor and still expect to be rewarded in heaven? Something is definitively wrong with this image or with the modern utilization structure of the tithe.

If the tithing system is not applicable today, does this mean that all of God's children should collaborate their efforts and strive to get the work done on a voluntary basis? Why has the spirit of voluntarism in reference to gospel dissemination almost disappeared in so many Protestant churches? Some people, particularly musicians, are demanding pay for their role or services (not all do). But why should they not be paid? The Levitical musicians were paid from the tithe or shared a portion of the tithe as their reward. And if that is acceptable, why shouldn't the elders, deacons etc. who do so much behind the scene and in the absence of the pastors be rewarded for their services?

The argument or rationale is made that such people are temporary workers with full-time jobs and have their inheritance in reference to owning lands, houses, retirement funds, social security and other types of funds etc., while ministers/pastors have dedicated their lives on a full-time basis to the work of the Lord. What difference does it make since all are contributing to the advancement of the cause and should be rewarded proportionally based on the amount of time and effort given. This idea will be pursued again based on the conclusion of this book.

Number of Tithes and Special Use Controversy

As the Israelites continued their journey through the wilderness, settling and assembling their tents and organizing their temporary settlements by tribes, as well as dismantling to move again, it appears that this was very laborious work. In this very large settlement of over a million people, there had to be sufficient space to accommodate that number of people while avoiding contamination etc.

The sanctuary also had to be transported and assembled at some strategic location for all to have relatively easy access to it. With no skyscrapers in which to live, there had to be a very large geographic area for any temporary settlement. And when they entered the Promised Land, the settlement would have been much more extensive in order for them to work the land and produce sufficient food to feed that great number of people.

Inherent in such a social organization, separation and settlement by tribe, the distance to the centralized place of worship would be significantly increased and some people would have to travel numerous miles on foot, by horse or other means of transportation for days and probably weeks to get to the place of worship. This means that on arrival, some of the produce set aside as tithes and offerings would have been spoiled or rotted, and rendered useless. A map of this settlement clearly indicates the long distances many would have to travel to present their tithe and offerings to the Levites and priests in the Sanctuary/Temple.

This dwelling place for God's presence amongst His people was the sanctuary and He instructed them

> *". . . to seek the place the Lord your God will choose from among your tribes to put his name there for his dwelling; there bring your burnt offerings and sacrifices, your tithes and special gifts, what you have vowed to give and your freewill offerings, and the firstborn of your herds and flocks" (Deut. 12:5, 6).*

As was mentioned earlier, the same social arrangement and or structural division by tribe were maintained after the Israelites crossed over the Jordan River into the Promised Land. In Deuteronomy 12:10-21, Israel was instructed that *". . .when ye go over the Jordan, and dwell in the land which the Lord your God giveth you to inherit," (vs.10),* they were to carry their tithes and offerings to the place specified in verse eleven, the sanctuary, and rejoice before the Lord. However, regardless of the distance that one lived from the sanctuary, the tithes and burnt offerings could not be offered anywhere but that central location where the Lord's name was established (vs. 13, 14).

It is in this same chapter that the idea of tithe consumption by tithe payers is introduced (vs. 17-19) while the burnt offerings were to be offered on the altar of the Lord according to verses 26 and 27. That which appears to be a contradiction and very controversial is found in Chapter 14:22-29. Verse 22 begins with the setting aside of the tithe *"...of all that your fields produce each year";* then verse 23 introduces that which seems contrary to the Lord's command in reference to the use of the tithe. *"Eat the tithe of your grain, new wine and oil, and the first born of your herds and flocks in the presence of the Lord your God at the place he will choose as a dwelling for his Name so that you may learn to revere the Lord your God always" (vs. 23).* Verses 24-27 give some indication as to the reason for the personal consumption of the tithe as well as the tithe conversion to money for its preservation on the trip to the Sanctuary.

> *"But if that place is too distant and you have been blessed by the Lord your God and cannot carry your tithe (because the place where the Lord will choose to put his Name is so far away), then exchange your tithe for silver, and take the silver with you and go to the place the Lord your God will choose. Use the silver to buy whatever you like: cattle, sheep, wine or other fermented drink, or anything you wish. Then you and your household shall eat there in*

the presence of the Lord your God and rejoice. And do not neglect the Levites living in your towns, for they have no allotment or inheritance of their own" (Deut. 14:24-27, NIV).

It is unfortunate that nothing is stated in the verse to give the exchanged tithe to the Levites and priests. That which is clear is that the money or silver is to be used to buy food products for the purpose of eating and rejoicing before the Lord. However, that which appears to be very significant in these verses is the logistics of transporting the tithes (it was an agricultural economy) of all the produce would have been extremely difficult and may be virtually impossible for those living at great distances from the sanctuary.

The tithe was in the form of reaped food products and live animals, and the time involved in traveling those distances would be insufficient for them, especially the produce, to arrive at the sanctuary location before spoilage set in, making the produce useless, unconsumable and a huge waste. In addition and for some people, the volume of the tithe may have been too great and impossible to transport. Thus, the common sense approach to convert it into cash/silver and take it to the sanctuary. But why consume it and rejoice before the Lord?

The idea of tithe conversion to silver seems appropriate, but the use of the silver to purchase food of any kind for the tithe payers' consumption with family members and Levites appears to be at the heart of the controversy. Some people and denominations believe that the tithe mentioned for this purpose is not the one that is exclusively allocated for the Levites and priests which is referred to as the first tithe.

It is suggested that Moses was referring to a second tithe provided by God for orphans, the poor, strangers etc. which seems to suggest that these people were not holy enough to eat of the first tithe even if this was God's demand/command.

Fortunately or unfortunately, the second tithe concept seems to have some validity or merit based on the book, Jewish History (vol. 1, p. 1003) written by Josephus. He went as far as mentioning a second and third tithe in the Jewish economy. However, his suggestion and that of others is not supported by:

- the direct and original instructions given by God to Moses or Aaron in reference to types of tithes since only one was mentioned, a tenth of all their produce etc., and
- any linguistic evidence in any of the texts written by Moses.

There are two fundamental Hebrew words used for tithe in the Pentateuch and other Old Testament books. One is first used in Genesis 28:22 by Jacob when he promised to return one-tenth of his possessions to the Lord if the Lord accompanied him home safely; also in Deut. 14:22, 26:12 for a mandatory tithe given under the law; Neh. 10:37,38 and 1Samuel 8:15,17 in which Samuel used the same word to describe taxes imposed by a king. The pivotal Hebrew word transliteration is "asar" and it is a verb meaning "to give a tenth part, to take a tenth part, to give the tithe, to receive the tithe" (The Complete Word Study Dictionary, Old Testament, 2003, p. 879). And the other word used by Moses and other O.T. writers is "maser" which is a masculine noun and its meaning is tithe or a tenth. "It is related to eser, meaning ten, and often means tenth (Gen. 14:20); Eze. 45:11, 14). In the Levitical system of the Old Testament, this word refers to the tenth part, which came to be known as the tithe." (Ibid.)

The expectation was that the Israelites were to tithe from their land, herds, flocks and other sources, and these tithes were intended for the support of the Levites and priests (Numbers 18:21, 24, 26, 28**)** *"...as well as strangers, orphans and widows" (Deut. 26:12;* Ibid. p. 648**)**. It cannot be overemphasized that from a linguistic perspective, there is no distinction made between the originally prescribed tithe(s) and any other tithe. There is also no suggestive language from which one can assume there was a second and third tithe prescribed by God to Moses or Aaron. Unless there is some grammatical construction in the Hebrew language that provides a different contextual meaning of the words used that will demonstrate the addition of a second and third tithe of which the author is unaware.

It is interesting to note that the same Hebrew word used to describe the tithe in Leviticus 27:36-37 is also used in Numbers 18:21, 24, 26, 28, and the same tithe is used for strangers, orphans and widows in Deuteronomy 26:12 as is stated above. The assertion and or assumption, that the tithe mentioned for these categories of people could not be the one designated for the exclusive use of the Levites and priests, has no linguistic support and appears to be invalid.

In addition, the Levites and priests were no more holy nor important than any other in Israel. They were given a functional role to perform and were rewarded with the tithe by God as a reward for their services. Their selection by God and assigned function did not make them angels in the sight of God or man. These were mere mortal beings with every human defect as those not chosen, and they offered sacrifices for their sins also. Even the High Priest had to do the same prior to entering the presence of God in the Most Holy Place. They made some very serious mistakes and or committed some pernicious sins (priests were killing other priests in order to inherit the more and most enviable portions of animal parts for their consumption) that not only corrupted the priesthood but brought it into a state of disrepute.

The significant point to remember is that all the tithe and offerings belonged to God and not to the Levites and priests. They were God's and He gave them to those workers. God is Sovereign King and Owner of everything and if He chose to give that which is His to the Levites and priests, he can choose to give them to any one for any purpose He sees fit. If He directed the Israelites to use the tithe or its silver conversion to purchase food for a feast that they may eat in His presence and rejoice; or to feed the aliens, orphans and widows, it is His prerogative to do so.

Why should we assume that because He first designated the tithe for a select few, that He could not use it to feed the "common people" who were not eligible to partake of it. What arrogance for us to assume that those who were selected to work in the sanctuary were placed in some special and enviable position for them to look down on those whom they served, or for them to exhibit an attitude of superiority because they were not of "common stock." The orphans. widows and strangers were probably in greater need of the tenth or tithe than those for whom it was slated.

There are certain life situations that require unconventional actions even when they appear to contravene certain established laws and principles. A similar situation was played out when David and his fighting men entered the Temple and ate the shewbread that was designated for the priest only (1 Samuel 21:6; Matthew 12:3, 4). This apparent law contravention act was accepted by God because it was intended to save lives and the life preservation principle is of greater value than any other designated for the daily sustenance of a select few.

The same holds true for the instructions given to the Israelites in Deuteronomy 14 and 26:12, 13 which state that,

> *"At the end of every three years, bring all the tithes of that year's produce and store it in your towns, so that the Levites (who have no allotment or inheritance of their own) and the aliens, the fatherless and the widows who live in your towns may come and eat and be satisfied, and so that the Lord your God may bless you in all the work of you hands.*
>
> *When you have finished setting aside a tenth of all your produce in the third year, the year of the tithe, you shall give it to the Levites, the alien, the fatherless and the widow, so that they may eat in your towns and be satisfied (vs. 12)*
>
> *Then say to the Lord your God: I have removed from my house the sacred portion and have given it to the Levite, the alien, the fatherless and the widow, according to all you commanded. . . ."*

These two passages are interpreted by some to mean that a third tenth or tithe was set aside every three years for this festive meal/feast. According to Unger 1975, p. 1103, *"That in every third year either this festival tithe or a third tenth was to be eaten in company with the poor and the Levites",* and he then ask if there were three tithes collected in the third year, or if the third one was *"only the second under a different description?"* He then concedes that the third tithe is *"not without support,"* and quoted the Jewish historian, Josephus, who mentioned three tithes in his writings. *"On the other hand, Maimonides says the third and sixth years second tithe was shared between the poor and the Levites, i.e., there was no third tithe."* And he concludes that *"of these opinions that which maintains three separate and complete tithing seem improbable."*

In addition, the Expositor's Commentary quotes Josephus (Antiq. 1V, 285,240-43 [Viii 8,227] as distinguishing these tithes, one for the Levites (Numbers 18:20-32); the second for the Israelites to eat and enjoy in a chosen place (Deuteronomy 14:22-7); and a third to be given every third year for the poor, the widows and orphans etc. (Deut. 14:28-9). And the book of Tobit 1:7-8 is also quoted in support of the three tithes:

> *"A tenth part of all my produce I would give to the sons of Levi, who officiated at Jerusalem, and another tenth I would sell and go and spend the proceeds in Jerusalem each year, and a third I would give to those to whom it was fitting to give it"*
> (Expositor's Bible Commentary, Vol. 3, P. 103).

Then the conclusion that follows is that "while this indicates that the three tithes were known in the second century B.C., the second and third tithes are more freely interpreted than one might adduce from Deuteronomy; and this is not necessarily the correct interpretation of the data in Numbers and Deuteronomy" (Ibid. Vol. 3, p. 1030). Furthermore, a more concise and vivid conclusion is stated in reference to all three tithe conceptions in the following. ***"So all the designations of tithes speak of one basic tithe to be put to various uses"*** (Ibid. p. 102).

There may have been an evolution in reference to additional tithe conceptions over time in the history of Israel, but the original instructions given to Moses and Aaron for tithe paying do not include a second and or a third tithe. The word for tithe used in Deuteronomy 26:12, 13, the primary texts used to suggest a third tithe, is the same as was defined earlier. There is no distinction (adjectival, numerical or otherwise) made between the first or original tenth and the assumed second and third, they are all one and the same. This means, as was also mentioned earlier, that God, the Sovereign King, Ruler and Owner, can designate its use for any purpose or can give it to any one person or group of people He wants His portion assigned. The tithe is/was sacred, not because the people for whom it was allotted were holy, but because God made it holy and gave it to those whom He selected to carry on His mediatorial work with the human family. The tithe being made holy by God does not transfer its sanctity/holiness to those who use it because it cannot sanctify anyone. It is God's and given to those who do His work as a reward/payment.

Tithing in the Promised Land

On numerous occasions in the Promised Land, Israel neglected its obligation in reference to the tithing law. Surprisingly enough, not even during the reign of the wisest man and king, Solomon, is anything mentioned about tithing. As a consequence of the neglect (and particularly when Israel sinned and God permitted foreign nations to capture and or slaughter Judah and Israel), the Levites and priests were left with no sanctuary/temple in which to perform their assigned duties and resorted to working in the fields to support themselves. There are other times when the Israelites consciously violated the tithing law and the sanctuary fell into disrepair.

A good example is found in 2Chronicle 28-31 in which King Ahaz apostatized. He completely turned away from the God of Israel and worshipped false gods, made ungodly sacrifices and eventually *". . .took some of the things from the temple of the Lord and from the royal and from the princes and presented them to the king of Assyria, but that did not help him"* (2Chron. 28:21). Eventually, he died and the great reformer, King Hezekiah, succeeded him as king in Jerusalem. According to 2Chronicles 29:1-7, He repaired the temple and restored every aspect of the sanctuary worship. He did that which was right in the sight of God (read 2Chron. 29-31). King Hezekiah contributed in significant ways of his possessions for the morning and evening burnt offerings, and

"He ordered the people living in Jerusalem to give the portion due to the priests and Levites so they

could devote themselves to the Law of the Lord. As soon as the order went out, the Israelites generously gave the first fruits of their grains, new wine, oil and honey and all that the fields produced. They brought a great amount, a tithe of everything" (2Chronincles 31;4, 5, NIV).

The temple and its services restoration caught on or was made known both in Israel and Judah since the men who lived there **". . .also brought a tithe of their herds and flock and a tithe of the holy things dedicated to the Lord their God, and they piled them in heaps"** (vs. 6). There was such great abundance of produce/products brought to the temple that the king requested the preparation of a *storehouse/storerooms* in the temple for the accommodation of all the tithe and offerings. *For the first time, probably, in the history of the temple/sanctuary, it was ordered to construct/add a storeroom to house all the tithes and offerings, and Levitical officials were appointed and paid from the tithe to take charge of all that were placed in the storerooms (2 Chronicles 31:11-15).*

The other significant reform in reference to tithe paying and offerings was after the people, Israelites, *". . .came up from the captivity of the exiles whom Nebuchadnezzar king of Babylon had taken captive (they returned to Jerusalem and Judah, each to his own town in company with . . .)"* (Nehemiah7:6, NIV). They rebuilt the walls of Jerusalem, restored the sanctuary and reorganized themselves for normal living. Men were again *". . .appointed to be in charge of the storerooms for the contributions, firstfruits and tithes"* (Neh.

12:44, NIV), and the walls were dedicated, and there was much singing and rejoicing. For further information on Nehemiah's reforms, read chapter 13 of the said book.

That which is noteworthy here is no change in terms of the Levites collecting the tithes, and giving one-tenth to the priests. However, when the collection was conducted, *"...the priest the son of Aaron..."* *was present with them but he did not take the one-tenth of the* *tithes, "...the Levites shall bring up the tithe of the tithes unto the* *house of our God, to the chambers, into the treasure house"* (Neh. 10:38, KJV).

The great intrigue is the presence of a priest when the tithes were collected. Why was he present? Is it that the Levites came under suspicion for not reporting and or giving an honest tithe to the priests? The reason is not given but it seems very unusual for this to have occurred particularly when one understands that it was not the responsibility of the priests to be present to collect their portion of the tithe when it was collected by the Levites on the site or place of collection.

In addition, the concept of non-priests or Levites collecting the tithe from the people and keeping ninety percent of it for themselves as a reward for their services in the Temple, while paying ten percent of the one-tenth to the priests, is a confirmation of the original purpose of the tithe and its structural distribution. And as should be noted, the words used for tithes in this book are the same used previously in Numbers and Deuteronomy, and no linguistic indication is presented to introduce and or confirm a second or third tithe.

There is a brief mention in Amos 4:4 about **"...tithes every three** **years"** which seems to have some link to Deut. 11:28; 26:12. Again, the language, and more specifically, the word used for tithes does not suggest a difference from the regular or first ten percent. In other words, there is no clear indication that a "second" and "third" tithes were prescribed for certain non–Levitical/clerical things and that they were different from the original tithe(s).

The final mention of tithe or tithe paying is found in the last book of the Old Testament, Malachi. It does appear that the prophet Malachi was a contemporary of Nehemiah and may have been referring to the same situations in Judah after Nehemiah returned to the Persian king during which time there was great unfaithfulness on the part of the Israelites. The people were offering defective animals as sacrifices which were rejected by God. The priesthood became very corrupted and their teachings caused many to go astray. They had violated God's covenant with the Levites and God was exceptionally displeased with them. Having stated what God would do to them, he admonished repentance and a return to God. Chapter 3:7-10 (NIV) reads:

> *Ever since the time of your forefathers you have turned away from my decrees and have not kept them. Return to me, and I will return to you, says the Lord Almighty.*
>
> > *But you ask, 'How are we to return?'*
> > *Will a man rob God? Yet you rob me.*
> > *But you; ask, 'How do we rob you?'*
> > *In tithes and offerings.*
> > *You are under a curse - the whole nation of you*
> *- because you are robbing me.*

> ***Bring the whole tithe into the storehouse . . . .***
> ***Test me in this, says the Lord Almighty, and see if***
> ***I will not throw open the floodgates of heaven and***
> ***pour out so much blessing that you will not have***
> ***room enough for it.***"

What is of great interest here are: (1) the returning of the tithe is now associated with abundant blessing from the Lord, a type of carrot-and–stick approach, and (2) the introduction of the concept of theft if the tithe is not returned to Him. When God instituted and or introduced the tithing system to Moses and Aaron, there were no strings of blessings attached. There seemed to have been the understanding that God was the Sovereign Owner of everything and His propositions were accepted without question. He wanted the tribe of Levi and the male family members of the household of Aaron and his father to be priests in order to perform certain sacred functions in the sanctuary, and He instructed that a tithe be presented to them as a payment for their services and it was done. He had the authority to have requested a greater percentage and it would have been honored because of who He is. And the real beneficiaries of His proposal are the people for whom He instituted the system of worship.

God does not need our means to sustain Himself, it is used for the benefit of the human family. We should, therefore, not be encouraged to give any portion of our finances, time, talents etc. in the service of God on condition of what He will do in return for us. We should do so because we love Him and our fellowmen, the latter of whom are the real beneficiaries, and because our Lord has directed it to be done.

It should be noted here that blessings come not by one's simple adherence to God's commands, but by one's faithfulness, obedience and loyalty to Him. There may be an inherent technicality in this statement, but I justify it by suggesting that if we give based on some ulterior motive such as giving to get or giving as a show, the gift will not be acceptable to God. Giving must be done with the right motive and spirit. There are some proponents who believe that regardless of the motive involved, the blessings will flow on the basis of our obedience to the command of God. The point is not to pass judgment on anyone and his/her motive for giving because no human being can enter into the mind of God to see absolutely what His thoughts are and on what basis(es) He chooses when He decides to bless someone whom we think is not deserving. It is an area from which we should all extract ourselves and let the Divine work without questioning.

In addition, the concept of robbery or robbing God is linked to His people's unfaithfulness in not adhering to His tithing command. Some Western-oriented-thinking people may be inclined to think of the definition of robbery within their cultural/legal persuasion and conclude that one's rejection of the O.T. tithing law is certainly not an act of robbery. Let us examine a legal situation with which we are generally acquainted.

Many governments extract without our individual permission, and painfully so at times, fifteen, twenty, thirty, forty percent of our gross income, and there is no legal recourse for this "illegal" action to those who hate paying taxes. Many people hire tax attorneys to assist them in finding as many loop holes in the tax laws to circumvent paying their fair share of taxes. Some just do not pay and when they are caught, drastic measures are exacted against them to extract the unpaid taxes, and some find themselves in certain institutions where their total lives are directed by others while their earthly possessions are confiscated by governments. The latter are referred to as tax cheaters and "thieves" even though they did not steel nor take anything illegally from those governments. From a legal perspective, anyone who should have paid taxes and did not is considered a thief or tax cheat. So one does not have to take something from another without that person's permission to be considered a thief from a biblical perspective.

I can understand, therefore, the reason for the robbery concept addition/attachment, but the motive for so doing is not clear. I can only hope that this approach was not a scare tactic use to impress on the minds of the people the outpouring of the wrath of God on all those who selected to violate the tithing law. God wants us to be faithful to Him because we love Him. He does not use force nor scare tactics to woo us to Him. He loves us dearly and sincerely, and desires us to do the same in return.

Gross or Net?

A very significant issue that is related to the O.T. tithing precept but seems not to have been an issue then, is whether those Christians who believe in the validity of the tithing principle should base their tithe on their gross or net income? It is a serious question with which many Christians wrestle, some for a life time.

A close examination of the tithing passages in the O.T. (an agri-cultural economy) seems to suggest that the tithe of produce etc. was based on the total yield of the crop without any deduction, not even the value of the seeds or seedlings acquired to plant the crop. This arrangement was based on a simple economy with no government taxes and other family and business expenses. The simple conclusion, based on the O.T. passages, is that tithe paying was based on the gross.

In a modern and much more complex society, would God allow for the enormous expenses incurred involuntarily and voluntarily by Christians? The mandatory Federal, state, county, city, sales and other "investment" taxes create a tremendous burden on numerous Christians. And the real-life living expenses such as mortgage, rent, gas, oil to heat homes during the winter months, food, clothing, medical and other insurance charges, union dues, transportation, furniture cost are all expenses that cannot be overlooked in our modern culture.

Would it be appropriate to make all these deductions and base the tithe on that which remains? Or would God allow for the cost incurred in reference to all that is invested for work purposes such as clothe, transportation and gas before the tithe is calculated? Modern businesses are allowed to make several deductions in reference to their operational cost before taxes are calculated by governments. If governments are that calculatingly empathetic, what would God do for His people today? If, however, you believe in the O.T. tithing principle, there seems to be no way out except to accept the bare facts about this precept as is outlined.

However, I am convinced that God would allow for the deduction of all investment cost for businesses prior to the tithing of their profits in our modern and very complex economy. Does the same hold true for each family? And is family considered to be a business? There are

72

some families that incorporate, and would the same deductions be appropriate for those families and not for those who do not incorporate? Pray to God for wisdom and ask the Spirit to guide you in making such determinations.

Retirement

There are some retirees who believe that because they are on a fixed income, they are not required to pay tithe. If you believe in the O.T. tithing law, you are to return the tithe since the money you collect is considered income and subject to be tithed. If, however, the income you receive is not subject to be tithed because you have already paid tithe on your gross income so that deduction (SS) which is coming back to you should not be tithed again.

This is suggested based on the assumption that the income was tithed if you paid it on the gross of your income. However, if one is retired for a very long time and is getting back from Social Security more than what was paid in, how does one decide when to start paying tithe on the extra portion on which tithe was not paid? In other words, if you cannot determine whether or not tithe was paid in full on the current SS income, what are the options available to decide what to return? I am convinced that there are times when people become too legalistic about the fine print implementation and end up losing out on the blessings. Let the Holy Spirit lead you under such circumstances.

Gifts

There are some people who believe that gifts are considered to be increases and subject to be tithed. If one receives a monetary gift, it would be much easier to calculate the exact tithe. However, if the gift is non-monetary, one may decide to place a monetary value on the gift and then pay tithe on the value. The important question is, should tithe be returned on any or all gifts, and what is the size or value of a gift that should trigger a tithe assessment?

Let us assume that a mother passes down to her daughter on her wedding day a precious family possession such as a very expensive gold ring or some other priceless valuable, should the receiver have the items appraised and then pay a tithe on the gift? How about the scenario that the mother who inherited the same gift had already returned a tithe on the gift, should the daughter then be compelled by conscience to do the same? If the item was tithed twice or more times, would the Spirit influence the daughter to exclude returning tithes on the gift? And if not, would she be entitled to a refund?

The avoidance of such legalistic minutiae is what Jesus warned against in His address to the Pharisees about paying tithe of mint etc. Making such determinations can become so mentally burdensome, energy taxing and so time consuming that the weightier matters of the law and life are neglected. If you are led by the Spirit to return a tithe on a gift, do so, and if you are not convinced, do not. If you stay in close communion with the Spirit and pray for wisdom and His direction, it will be forthcoming. Do not beat up yourself and lose the blessings God has in store for you.

Conclusion

Many have alluded to the idea that the tithing system was in existence prior to its institution by God in Israel according to the book of Numbers. They generally point to Abram (Abraham) paying a tithe of his war spoil to Melchezidek, King and Priest of Salem in Genesis 14:20, and Jacob's promise to give the Lord a tenth of all that God will give him for a safe journey and return to his father's house in Genesis 28:22.

It does appear that some semblance of a sacrificial system was in existence prior to its institutionalization in Israel after her liberation from Egypt. Evidence of animal sacrifice is evidenced by Abel and numerous others, and the sacrificial act was executed by the patriarchal heads of families. It also appears that God's children were few in number from creation to the time of Joseph being sold in Egypt and Jacob (Joseph's father), and the entire family joining him there. Even during Noah's time, only he and his family were saved in the ark. There seems to be no evidence of the existence of an organized Jehovah's priesthood/priests to whom the tithes would have been paid prior to the introduction of the tithing system by God in Israel. If there was an established tithing system as some contend, to whom was the tithes paid or for what purpose was it used.

One thing is clear and that is, God Himself instituted the tithing system in Israel. It was revealed to Moses and Aaron as the economic engine for the support of the sacrificial system of worship in the sanctuary. He selected the Tribe of Levi and gave them the tithe of all the produce as their wage or payment for their services in the Temple/

sanctuary. They were to care for the temple and assist the priests in the execution of their role. They could not be priests nor could they perform the functions of the priests. There were clear demarcations in reference to the roles of Levis and priests. And they were to give a tenth of the tithe to the priests

On the other hand, the priests were appointed by God and only Aaron and his father, and their male descendants could be priests. In other words, although these families were from the Tribe of Levi, only they were given the priesthood and allowed to collect a tenth of all the tithes collected by the Levites, as well as the animal offerings etc. Their role performance at the altar was separate and distinct from those of the other Levites. However, both Levites and priests were appointed by God and the tithes and offerings were given to them because they were expected to perform their duties on a full-time basis. They had no other inheritance and should not be distracted by any other type of work.

The one thing that seems to be exceptionally clear is that the tithing law was not instituted as a separate and independent entity from the sacrificial system as some contend, even though there may have been such a practice of giving a tenth or a tithe on certain prior occasions. This, however, is not a sound or sufficient basis on which to claim that its independent establishment provided immunity or exclusion from its abrogation with the whole sacrificial system when Christ died on the cross. Otherwise, a similar argument could be made for the sacrificial sin offerings that were also instituted independently of and prior to the sacrificial institution, but was made obsolete at the cross.

They were combined and institutionalized by God as one system. For the sacrificial system of worship to work in Israel as God intended it, the tithing law was a necessary economic support that was inter-twined into the fabric of the system for its effective and efficient operation. In other words, if one aspect or component failed, tithing or priesthood, the whole system would disintegrate as was evidenced earlier in Israel when they refused to comply with the tithing principle. One may believe that the sacrificial system was not dependent on the tithing precept since it was introduced much earlier and functioned independently of the former.

This is true, but with the institutionalization of the sacrificial system and the man power (priests and Levites) needed to operate it on a full-time basis, an economic system was needed to support such an operation on that large scale and God chose and included the tithing concept for that purpose. He did not rely on the voluntarism of people. In order to ascertain their presence in the Temple when they were needed, He paid them to be present and they were there. If He had allowed them to be involved in any other line of work, they would have had a plausible excuse at times and this would have been detrimental to the effectiveness and efficiency of the sanctuary services. What a wise God we serve.

It can be concluded that the sanctuary, priesthood, Levitical assistants, sacrificial offerings, the tithing law and all the other cer-emonial laws were inextricably combined into one institution. The tithing system was designed and applied to the sacrificial system of worship by God. This is understandable since the establishment of an institution, with the expectation of its mission effectuation inherent in its plan, will include a uniquely structured or planned financial system for the support of its operations. In other words, such an economic arrangement will have little or no relevance and be non-transferable to another system that is structurally different without significant changes.

The bottom line is that the sacrificial system in its totality was fundamentally a system of imperfect symbolisms pointing to the real and perfect sacrificial Lamb of God revealed in Jesus Christ dying on the cross for the redemption of the human family. Does this mean that when Christ died on the cross, the sacrificial system, including the tithing law, was abrogated? Or did the tithing precept survive its abolition with the sacrificial system? These are critical questions that will be addressed in the next chapter. So we turn our attention to the teaching of Jesus and other New Testament writers on the sacrificial and tithing laws.

Chapter II

Tithing in the New Testament

It is very regrettable and exceptionally unfortunate that so much theological extrapolation has been made in reference to statements by certain authors about the early Christians or New Testament church members paying tithes and offerings as we know them in the twenty-first century. Were the early Christians really paying tithes and offerings? If this is the case, where is the scriptural evidence? Is there any linguistic and or extra-biblical documentation that can support positively such a claim or conclusion? Or are the extrapolations made as a justification for the continuation of the present system of tithing and offerings? This concept of tithing and offerings will be closely scrutinized through an examination of all the significant New Testament passages of scripture used to prop up or support the continued existence and implementation of the tithing principle in the New Dispensation by many Protestant churches.

Christians must clearly understand that there is a theological continuation between the Old Testament and the New Testament but that there is also a substantial divide between them. The great divide began with the birth of Jesus and was consummated with His death on the cross, His resurrection and ascension as our King and High Priest in the heavenly abode. As a result of His coming to earth and effectuating gloriously His mission, many significant changes were introduced and slowly implemented over time. One such major and instantaneous change was the dissolution of the sacrificial system of worship and all the trappings or laws associated with it, including the exclusive Aaronic family priesthood and apparently, the economic system instituted for its support. So if Christians in the N.T. time were paying tithes and offerings, to whom were they paying them when the positions and functions of the priests and Levites were annulled or no longer valid and therefore irrelevant in the Christian era?

At this juncture, however, it is necessary to recap some of the important ideas mentioned and worth remembering in the previous chapter before we proceed. There is no doubt to the person of faith (Christian) that God instituted the sacrificial system with the tithing/ offerings components (including sacrificial offerings), as the sole economic engine to keep it going/operating. Its significant connection to and interdependence with the system of worship in His sanctuary is clearly demonstrated when the eleven tribes decided to contravene the tithing law by withholding their tithes from the Levites. This negative action forced the Levites and priests to abandon their daily sanctuary duties in order to work in the fields to earn a living while the place of worship lapsed into a state of decay or disrepair (Nehemiah 13:10, 11).

It should be reiterated here that the Levites and the Aaronic priests were directly appointed by God for the execution of very distinctly separate roles in His sanctuary. The Levites were not priests and could not cross over into the priesthood in spite of their Levitical genealogy. Only Aaron and his father's family members (males and their male descendents) could be priests out of the entire tribe of Levi (some 22,000 members), and meticulous records were kept to ascertain the genealogical purity of the priesthood down through the ages in temple history. These historical records remained intact until the complete destruction of Jerusalem in A.D. 70 by the Roman Empire. More will be written about the impact of this disastrous catastrophe.

Such a divinely majestic system of worship was designed, however, to be a temporary and symbolic medium pointing to the real sacrificial Lamb of God, Jesus Christ, dying on the cross in fulfillment of His earthly mission. If this is the case or true reality, does this mean that the sacrificial system or any aspect of it crossed over from the Old Testament into the New Dispensation and is still valid for Christians today? Or does it mean that only one of the structural components of the worship services (the tithing law) has validity and applicability in the Christian era? And is there any other aspect of the sacrificial system that is also transferable to the New Dispensation?

Some people believe that the sacrificial aspect of the system was invalidated at the cross while its economic engine was spared and is applicable in the Christian Dispensation. Let us turn our attention to a rigorously objective examination of the New Testament passages of scripture used by many as a verification and or justifiable support for the continued existence and implementation of the tithing law in the New Dispensation.

Those passages that directly mention the word "tithe" will be dealt with first followed by the others. In other words, they all will not be dealt with in sequential order of appearance in the N.T.

N. T. Scriptural Passages Used to Support The Tithing Principle.

There are few textual passages that deal with or mention the word "tithe" in the New Testament. The following one is a quintessential example of those use as a direct and or indirect instruction for the transference and application of the O.T. tithing law and or practice to that of the New Dispensation.

> **Matthew 23:23 (corresponding text is Luke 11:42)**
> *– "Woe to you, teachers of the law and Pharisees, you hypocrites! You give a tenth of your spices – mint, dill and cumin. But you have neglected the more important matters of the law – justice, mercy and faithfulness. You should have practiced the latter, without neglecting the former." (NIV).*

This is by far, one of the most quoted N.T. scriptural passages used in reference to Jesus' validation of the tithing principle. But how much weight does it really carry to tithing confirmation in the New Dispensation or after the death of Christ? Let us examine it within its context.

Verse one of this said chapter (the one mentioned above) gives the context in which Jesus candidly criticized the teachers of the law and the Pharisees. He was addressing a crowd of people and His disciples, when He mentioned the contradictory behavior of these religious and very important Jewish leaders. It is assumed that the same teachers of the law and Pharisees were present in the said crowd and His criticism was quite severe in regards to their hypocritical and contra-dictory lifestyles. The said criticism was fundamentally about their unscrupulous meticulosity in paying tithe of the smallest herbs while neglecting principles of greater significance in the law. Their legalistic behavior in this particular matter appears to be a hallow sham of keeping or adhering to the external in order to gain some merits or brownie points from God while ignoring those internally significant principles of the law.

It should be stated unequivocally that Jesus did not condemn the paying of tithe on these miniscule items (although they were excluded from the original produce to be tithed) with His very severe criticism of these men. It was the emphasis that they placed on the public display of tithing while their behavioral attitude toward other human beings fell notably short of adhering to the important principles of justice, mercy etc., and this was deplorable or did not measure up to the high standards of God's expectations.

Jesus' statement also appears to have confirmed the current adherence to the tithing law when He said that *". . .you should have practiced the latter without neglecting the former"* (Ibid.). This affirmation gives credence to the tithing system in Jesus' time since the sacrificial system of worship was still in existence and valid due to the fact that the sacrificial Lamb of God was yet to be slain or crucified on the cross. This is critical to bear in mind as we continue our examination of the other texts.

One cannot ignore, however, the implied minimization of tithe paying in the statement which seems to suggest a type of hierarchical level of importance placed on certain biblical principles. The suggestion is that paying tithe was important but not as significant as the other principles of the moral law mentioned by Christ. The essence of what Jesus was conveying appears to be that the Pharisees extended too much zeal/mental energy on the trifles or small things of the law that left them with a very minute amount of or no time and motivation for the effectuation of the weightier matters of the law in their lives. Implied legalism?

Legalism is a reality concept about which all Christians should be very concerned. Its practice can distort extensively one's perception by adding blinders to the mind's eye and so empty or drain an individual's energy to the point where it may not be able to be replenished. This will inevitably leave one with little or no motivation or enthusiasm for the significant matters of practical Christianity. It can also be transferred to one's life possessions as is revealed in a story I read about in which some Pharisee-related family members trained their oxen to withhold their labor from working the land if tithe was not submitted from its produce. When the animals withheld their labor or stopped working in response to the unfaithfulness of their owners in not returning a faithful tithe, the owners were shocked and wondered about the reason for the animals' behavioral display until it dawned upon them as to how they had trained their animals or oxen.

In addition, the Greek word used by Jesus in this context and the one in Luke 11:42 is "**apodekatoo**" which means "to pay or give tithes" or a tenth as was stated in the O.T. In other words, Jesus in His statement did not depart by adding or subtracting anything or aspect of the O.T. tithe. It was the same word He used in the Parable of the Pharisee and the Tax Collector in Luke 18:10-14.

> **Luke 18:11, 12 –**
>
> *"The Pharisee stood up and prayed about himself: 'God, I thank you that I am not like other men – robbers, evildoers, adulterers – or even this tax collector. I fast twice a week and give a tenth of all I get."*

Jesus mentioned the word for tenth or tithe in the above text and in the context of comparing the contemptuous, self-righteous and self-confident attitude of those first-century Pharisees who performed certain public acts in order to be in the graces of God and man, while failing to comprehend that righteousness comes only from God and not from external works, including tithe paying. But the humble attitude of the tax collector who did not plead his good works sought the mercy of God in forgiving his sins.

It can be assumed that Jesus mentioned the tenth or tithe paid by the Pharisees because this is one of the major things with which they were unscrupulously exacting, yet very minor in nature as compared with other biblical principles. In other words, tithe paying was one of the things with which they, the Pharisees, were identified. Jesus did not use it, the tenth, in a manner as to disaffirm it, since it was still a "legally" binding practice up to the point in time when it was mentioned by Him, and even to the time of His death. So were the other ritualistic practices such as the one He recommended to the healed leper to go and show himself to the priest and give the required offering. This is a validation of the O.T. priesthood by Christ which became obsolete at the time of His death also.

As was mentioned earlier, the Prophet Malachi portrays the negligence of or the willful defiance of not returning the tithe as an act of robbing God or stealing from Him which is a contravention of both the tithing law and the moral law (thou shalt not steal), and would be classified and or considered as an unethical and down right immoral act. Yet in all of His sermons and or lectures/teachings, Jesus did not present any direct teaching on the subject matter. Is it that such a lack of direct instruction on tithing by Him may have been a consequence of the widespread, well established theological teachings, and practice on this subject matter that it was not a necessity to even mention it in any discussion or dialogue?

If this is the case for pedagogy, then why is there no biblical reference/record or evidence of Jesus or His disciples paying tithe on anything they earned or received as gifts if this was such a critically religious practice for the maintenance of the sacrificial system in Judaism and a carryover to Christianity in the New Dispensation? Or is the absence of such information linked to the imminent end of the old symbolisms that pointed to the coming of Christ and the inevitable abrogation of the sacrificial system that was in part slowly phased out in preparation for the new Christian era and therefore, no need to emphasize the old but to slowly introduce its replacement?

It is so difficult to determine why Jesus did not publicly emphasize tithe paying or why there is no biblical record of Him or His disciples paying tithe before or after His death. Such direct teaching and or record of such a practice would have made it easier to do as Jesus did. Any such teachings and or actions on this subject matter before His death would bring us to another question as to whether the tithing law was also annulled with the priesthood and sacrificial laws when He died on the cross?

That which Jesus did, appears to be a clear indication of His intentions and or the directions in which He desired His followers/disciples to go. In Luke 8:1-3, Jesus and His disciples travelled through many cities and villages preaching the good news of the kingdom of God, and Mary Magdalene, Joanna and Susanna, *"... and many others, which ministered unto him of their substance."*

Jesus and His disciples were very human and had to eat in order to live. They did not have the time to plant seeds and wait for the harvest to arrive. Jesus and His disciples did not collect tithes and would have been considered as religious rouges if they attempted to do so due to the fact that they were not connected genealogically to the Levi tribe or to Aaron's or his father's family. They, therefore, had no legitimate right to collect tithe from anyone in Israel. Strangely enough, Jesus is the Creator of the universe and man, but in human form, He was not connected to the tribe of Levi and had no right to the tithe and offerings collected by the Levites. So how were they to survive when they had no jobs from which they could receive a wage or salary?

In the above-mentioned passage, we are introduced to a few women who used their financial means and other resources to contribute to the needs of Jesus and His disciples. This charitable act appears to be a cultural custom in Israel for Israelites to contribute of their means to Rabbis. Women were not allowed to preach in Palestine, but many of them supported those who were involved in preaching the gospel. It also appears that there were many other people who supported Christ and His disciples in light of the fact that Judas was the individual who held the money bag and none of them worked, so from where did they acquire those funds used for their sustenance?

When the above passage with women supporting Jesus and His disciples is combined with or considered in light of what Jesus did in Matthew 10:5-10 and Luke 9:1-6, one begins to wonder if Jesus' instruction to His disciples established a pattern or basis for their operation then and in the future. And did He intend for the same instruction(s) to be the permanent precedence of operation to which all future disciples were bound to adhere in reference to how they should be supported in their gospel commission involvement? The following is what Jesus did.

He called His disciples and empowered them to heal the sick and raise the dead etc., and then He instructed them to ***"Provide neither gold, nor silver, nor brass in your purses, Nor scrip for your journey, neither two coats, neither shoes, nor yet staves: for the workman is worthy of his meat"*** (Mt. 10:9, 10 KJV). Luke reports that Jesus said, ***"Take nothing for your journey, neither staves, nor scrip, neither bread, neither money; neither have two coats apiece"*** (Luke 9:3, KJV).

These two passages of scripture refer to the same situation of Jesus calling His disciples and sending them to preach and heal etc. But why did He inform them to take nothing for their journey and become dependent on the benevolence of their fellow Jews that would have created tremendous uncertainty about their shelter and sustenance? Was it that they had to learn to truly trust or exercise their raw faith in Jesus with the assurance that He would never leave nor forsake them?

There is another passage of scripture in which Jesus appears to contradict His instructions not to take anything for the journey. It is Luke 22:35, 36 which states, "*... When I sent you without purse, and scrip, and shoes, lacked ye anything? And they said, Nothing.*

Then said he unto them, But now, he that hath a purse, let him take it, and likewise his scrip: and he that hath no sword, let him sell his garment, and buy one."

There are two critical ideas that all who are unaware should clearly understand and these are:

1.   According to the late William Barclay, it was absolutely forbidden for a Jewish Rabbi or teacher to accept any monetary value in exchange for teaching the Law to anyone except a child. Moses received freely the Law from God and all were expected to teach it to others free of any cost. No wonder Jesus reminded His disciples on that same occasion in Matthew 10:8, "*... freely ye have received, freely give.*" **(William Barclay, The Gospel of Matthew, Vol. 1, pp. 376-8).**

Jesus was their perfect Example as well as ours in reference to preaching, teaching and living out the principles of the kingdom of God without the acceptance of any monetary value for His service. He had also freely taught His disciples about the said principles of the kingdom of God and empowered them to preach, teach and heal etc. which they were about to do in His physical absence – without His presence and leadership – on their own, but empowered by the Spirit of God. They did not pay for their spiritual education, so why should they profit from their teaching of the same which may be considered gospel peddling?

This idea of not accepting any monetary value in exchange for preaching/teaching the Law of Moses was a well-established cultural norm that preceded Jesus' incarnation and was applied by Him as the norm of preaching/teaching the gospel of the kingdom of God within the said Jewish cultural context, and

2.   That which is of great interest in the above-mentioned words of Jesus is the implication in the following, *". . . the workman is worthy of his meat."* Without mentioning or going into the Greek etc., the workman (ergates) is the "laborer" or the one doing the work; "worthy" (axios) means deserving of, and "meat" (trophe) means food, sustenance and or nourishment. So if the workman, as a result of his labor, is deserving of food and he cannot accept any monetary value in exchange for preaching/teaching, who will provide him with such sustenance?

The answer is found in another cultural practice in which the Jewish community was duty bound to support any Rabbi due to the fact that he was neglecting his own affairs in order to concentrate on those of God. The question is, however, what is the implication for those who are involved in preaching/teaching the gospel of the kingdom of God on a full-time basis then and today? Again, the late William Barclay has concluded in his analysis of the said passage of scripture that *". . . the man of God must never be over-concerned with material things, but the people of God must never fail in their duty to see that the man of God receives a reasonable support. This is a passage which lays an obligation on teacher and on people alike"* (Ibid.).

The critical lesson, as was intimated previously, that Jesus was attempting to teach His disciples about not taking a purse on their money belt was for them to learn to be totally dependent on Him. If they were, although unspoken, He would impress on the minds of those being ministered to and others to take care of the material needs of His ministers and this is apparently what occurred. The answer to His question about lacking anything when they returned was that they lacked nothing. Lesson learned. Place your trust in and become completely dependent on Jesus and He will supply all your needs. This marvelous experience provided the necessary foundation on which the disciples could build in the future.

Does Jesus want us or His modern-day ministers to follow His instructions through the exercise of an unparalleled faith in Him in a time (the twenty-first century) and culture(s) that are so far removed from His day and culture? I know that the words of Jesus transcend time and culture, and that He wants us to be totally dependent on Him and the generosity of our spiritual brothers and sisters, and even strangers as we engage in the Gospel proclamation today. For those whose faith is not as deeply rooted or anchored in Jesus will have a difficult time moving forward without the assurance of a purse. So would a purse increase the faith of such people, and is this the type of faith that Jesus desires for His workers, one that is based on one's wallet or the material things of life?

Such people or workers may find some consolation in Jesus' other recommendation which appears to be a contradiction to take a purse or financial resources and scrip with them on future occasions. The issue for Neil Cole in reference to Jesus' teaching is not whether gospel workers are supported but when they are supported. He wrote, *"Going first in weakness and dependency is important. After people have shown they will do the work without support, we can support them more confidently. It's a testing process but much more than that. It is a growth process. . ."* (Organic Leadership, p.290). It is a reinforcement in the minds of those involved in gospel dissemination or other spiritual services, that Jesus is the God-man of His word and One Who can be trusted to deliver as promised?

The message for many who are serving in the cause of God today, and especially spiritual shepherd-servant leaders is that, *"If you're not willing to shepherd the flock without pay, then you're not qualified to do so for pay. If you can't lay your paycheck down for the sheep, you certainly won't lay your life down for them"* (ibid. 286).

That which is of greater importance to the author is, why is it that Jesus did not instruct His disciples to go and preach/teach the gospel of the kingdom of God and collect a tithe and offering from the people as a reward for their labor? Such an idea would have been futile and or met with great opposition because of the fact that His disciples were neither Levites nor priests and based on the law, had no legal right to the tithe and offerings. So was Jesus introducing, through the adoption of that Jewish cultural norm, a new method of financing the gospel commission for all Christians or full-time laborers? Before His death on the cross, the Levites and priests were "legally" collecting tithes and offerings from their brethren as a reward for their labor in the Temple, so why is it that Jesus did not inform His disciples about the transference and application of the tithing principle to the New Dispensation as the financial method for rewarding gospel laborers if this was His intention?

If anyone deserved the tithe, it was Jesus. According to the O.T. scripture, the tithe was His and He gave to the Levites. He was in a position to claim it for Himself and disciples, but being in human form, He adhered to the socio-religious norms and allowed the Levites and priests to continue ownership of the tithe and offerings until He died on the cross. No new law of ownership was articulated or written for the transfer of the tithe from the Levites and priests to any other person(s) or tribe(s). And based on the scriptural evidence presented so far, it does appear that the law of Levite-priest ownership was a component of the sacrificial laws that was nailed to the cross.

Before any definitive conclusion is made, however, let us examine the other N.T. passages on tithing to determine their meaning, intent, and relevance.

Hebrews 7:5, 6 (NIV) –

"Now the law requires the descendents of Levi who became priests to collect a tenth from the people – that is their brothers - even though their brothers are descendents from Abraham. This man,

however, did not trace his descent from Levi; yet he collected a tenth from Abraham and blessed him who had the promises."

This is another of the prominent passages of scripture that is quoted in many presentations as a justification for the survival of the tithing law at the cross and its implementation in the New Dispensation. It is understood that the tithing concept is mentioned here in a book that is part of the New Testament, but does the mention of tithe in this section of the Bible a clear indication of its applicability in the New Era? And does that mean the author's intention in the passages above is a convincing validation of its transference from the O.T. to the Christian era?

There is no question that Paul mentioned the words of a tenth or tithe in the above-written passage, but why did he refer to this O.T. tithing concept and what was his intention? If the above translation is correct, however, it raises a simplistic yet technical question in regards to the factual content of verse five. The descendants of Levi who became priests did not collect a tenth from the people according to the book of Numbers. The tithe was exclusively collected by the none-priestly members of the Tribe of Levi as a reward for their services in the temple, and they in turn shared and or presented a tenth of it to those who were appointed as priests. This is not a blunder of great significance and does not present a barrier to moving forward with the analysis.

Paul uses two Greek words for "tenth" which are "**apodekatoo**" which was also used by Jesus, and "**dekatoo**" that is used in verses 6 and 9 and means *"to receive tithes from"* (The Complete Word Study

Dictionary, N.T. , p. 404, 1993), and it appears to me that he was referencing the information from the book of Deuteronomy in which the tithing law was instituted. This means that both Jesus and Paul were referring to the said O.T. tithing system or practice that required Jews to provide a tenth of their produce etc. to the Levites as a reward for their services in the Sanctuary. But why did Paul refer to the Levitical priests receiving tithe from their brothers and present a type of comparison with Melchizedek receiving tithe from Abram even though he (Melchizedek) was not genealogically connected to the tribe of Levi? Was this tithe citing any indication for or an indirect teaching for the continuation of the practice in the Christian Dispensation by Paul as some believe? Understanding Paul's objective in this matter is of great significance.

He (Paul) was addressing the Jewish Christian converts who may have been very familiar with the O.T. teaching and were tempted to revert back to Judaism (NIV Bible p. 1857), and his task was to clearly and convincingly instruct/teach them about the supremacy and all-sufficiency of Jesus Christ as God's final revelation and in whom the prophecies and promises of the O.T. were fulfilled. In other words, Christ was superior to all prophets, angels, and priests, including Aaron the High Priest and all his descendents. It was His role, through His death, resurrection and ascension, to open the way to God that they were encouraged to look to as something of critical significance, because subsequent to His resurrection, Christ became the only High Priest and His position is far superior to any earthly High or regular priest. So even though the sacrificial system was still in existence in Judaism subsequent to Christ's death and resurrection due to the ignorance of the people in regards to the fulfillment of the Christocentric prophecies, Paul and the other disciples and Christians knew about the annulment of these things at the cross. Therefore, reverting back to Judaism would be futile because that system of worship has been made obsolete and has no real spiritual meaning or significance any more.

This new and apparently radical teaching may have been exceptionally difficult for them to comprehend due to the ingrained teachings of Moses and the divine institution of Aaron as High Priest, his father and their descendents as the only members in Judaism who could be High Priest and priests by law. And now you are proclaiming that Jesus who was not genealogically connected to the tribe of Levi is the most powerful High Priest. How could that be? Would that not entail the obsolescence of the old law and installation of a new one? Paul's main objective was to demonstrate to the Christian Jews that even though Jesus, the Son of God, was not connected in His humanity by tribal genes to Levi, but was after the order of Melchizedek, the King and priest of Salem, His priesthood was superior to that which preceded and or came after Him (they were only shadows and symbols representing Him, and pointing to His coming, the real and genuinely perfect sacrificial Lamb of God and High Priest). But how did he arrive at or on what theological reasoning or ground did he base his conclusion?

In Paul's (he is the assumed author or Hebrews) attempt to present a persuasive argumentation for the superiority of Christ's priesthood, he went back far into biblical history (Gen. 14:18-20) and cited the case of Melchizedek, King of Salem and priest of the most high God, going out to meet Abram as he returned from a victorious war with all his spoils and blessed as well as offered him (Abram) bread and wine. Abram, in turn, offered a tenth or tithe of the spoils to him. In verse four of chapter seven, it is written, *"Just think how great he was: Even the patriarch Abraham gave him a tenth of the plunder."* And in verses six and seven of the same chapter, it is stated that *"This man ... did not trace his descent from Levi, yet he collected a tenth from Abraham and blessed him who had the promise. And without doubt the lesser person is blessed by the greater."*

Based on this information in these passages, it is very clear that Abraham who is considered to be a very distinguished and honorable patriarch and prophet with a special promise from God is considered to be lesser than the king and priest of Salem, Melchizedek about whose ancestry little to nothing is known. Nothing is mentioned in the Bible about his father, mother, siblings nor extended family members etc. and he is considered to be (based on his office and or role) greater than Abraham, from whom he received the tithes. This situation is compared to the descendants of Levi who by law collected tithes from their brothers who were descendants of Abraham, which implies that the Levites (based on their office or role) were greater than their brothers. However, Christ's priesthood was not based on the imperfections of Aaron's but after the order of that non-Levitical mysterious figure and priesthood of Melchizedek. The point is that man's priesthood is imperfect and he eventually dies. Christ's priesthood could not have come from that of man's, He came through the Tribe of Judah, and His was based on that mysterious figure of Melchizedek who was considered to be a prefiguration of Christ.

Paul's citation of tithe in this scriptural context was neither a direct nor indirect teaching or confirmation of its validity and applicability in the Christian Dispensation. It was used to demonstrate how the lesser person(s) paid tithe to the greater and the legitimacy of the priesthood of Melchizedek to whom Abram supposedly paid tithe, yet he was not connected to nor was he a part of the family tree that preceded Levi. Jesus' priesthood followed or came after his, and although not connected to Levi, His priesthood was by far superior to the Aaronic and all subsequent priesthoods. It was in this historical context of demonstrating and or informing the Jewish Christians about the superiority of Christ's priesthood that tithing was mentioned. And it cannot be objectively stated that there is any linguistic evidence in these scriptural passages to support the paying of tithe since Paul's implicative intention was not to teach about the Christians' "legal" obligation to tithe paying but, as I mentioned before, to remind or teach the Hebrew Christians about the superiority of the priesthood of Christ.

There are many who still believe, however, that Paul was referencing or referring to the validity and applicability of tithing in the Christian era. If this is the case, why did he not state unequivocally the obligation of all Christians to continue the practice of paying tithes, not to earthly priests, but to Jesus Who is our heavenly High Priest due to the annulment of the Levitical priestly system at the cross? This would have been a grand contextual opportunity to remind and or instruct the Hebrew Christians of their spiritual obligation to continue the practice of tithe paying. But to whom would they pay it if the sacrificial system was no longer valid or extant, and the tithe and offerings were designated only for the Levites and priests, and the laws of their designation were annulled?

Fortunately or unfortunately, there is no direct nor indirect instructive information on tithing in the book of Hebrews to which one can legitimately refer as "legally" binding on any or all Christians. Any link, therefore, made from the O.T. tithing texts to the Book of Hebrews tithing references as definitive proof or evidence of the existence of the tithing law and the Christians' obligation to adhere to it, would be very disingenuous to say the least. As is written previously and in other words, the references were communicated to show the historical links in order to make plain or substantiate the significant change and focus from the earthly Levitical/Aronic priesthood to that of Christ's heavenly superior Priesthood.

We now turn to some other passages that are peripheral in nature but implies both tithing and stewardship principles. These are generally utilized to add some tangential support to the belief in the current validation of the tithing principle and the Christian obligation to adhere to it or not be blessed by God.

Matthew 19:21 – Jesus answered, *"If you want to be perfect, go, sell your possessions and give to the poor, and you will have treasure in heaven. Then come, follow me."*

In Jesus' encounter with the Rich Young Ruler, one critical and very obvious idea is observed and that is, Jesus did not instruct the young man to sell all his goods and give it to the temple priest or the Levites. He did not even inform him to sell and give a tithe of all to the Levites/priests since as a strict Jew, he would have paid his tithe. The instruction was to sell all, give it to the poor and then come and follow Jesus. What Christ wanted the young man to understand was that his legalistic adherence to the law was insufficient to attain his salvation. In other words, he could not earn his way into heaven. He had to fully surrender all that stood between him and God, and cling to Jesus, (He is grace), the only Way to eternal life. This text has nothing to do with tithing yet it is peripherally used in that context to support the principle.

A similar emphasis is noted in the mindset of the disciples when Jesus said to Judas, *"What you are about to do, do quickly"* (John 13:29). They did not comprehend why Jesus addressed those words to Judas and thought that because of his position as their treasurer, Jesus was *". . . telling him to buy what was needed for the feast, or to give something to the poor"* (vs. 29). Why would they even think in such a manner if there was not the mindset that was geared towards taking care of the poor which Jesus had done on numerous occasions. This trend towards caring for the poor is something that will be clearly seen later as a New Testament emphasis in this discussion and has no relevance to the tithing principle.

> ### Luke 6:38 –
>
> *"Give, and it shall be given unto you; good measure, pressed down, and shaken together, and running over, shall men give unto your bosom. For with the same measure that ye mete withal it shall be measured to you again."*

This is another text that is normally linked on the periphery to giving/tithing/stewardship. The verse is part of a speech Jesus gave to His disciples and a large crowd in which lessons were repeated from what is known as the Sermon on the Mount. Here Jesus reemphasized a fundamental principle of life which is *"what you sow is what you reap."* In other words, a farmer will never sow barley and reap oranges; nor will he/she sow tomatoes and reap potatoes; nor will one sow discord and reap harmony. What one gives of his/her accord and with good will, will be returned to the person in the same or some measure. This has no direct reference to tithing. In some indirect sense, it has some application and or relevance to the stewardship principle in reference to one's giving. The giver, however, should not give with this in mind. One does not give to the cause of God in order to be blessed or to get something in return. We should always remember that *"it is more blessed to give than to receive"* (Acts 20:35).

Giving in order to receive some favors or to get back the value of something in return for what was given or more is a very selfish motive. If that is the intention of the giver, why give in the first place, why not just keep what you have? I am convinced that God will reward us with blessings when our motives are right and giving comes from a willing heart.

A critical question in reference to the immediate text above is, if one does not give of one's accord or free will with a generous heart but based on a restrictive law in order to avoid the serious consequences associated with not giving, will the positive outcome of the principle of giving be realized? Some people believe that all one has to do is to obey the law, with or without the right motive, and the blessings are sure to follow. What if a person is not in position to give the "legally" required amount but gives what he/she can afford with a willing heart and with no expectation of any return, will that person be blessed also?

Difficult as these questions may be for us to answer positively since we do not have access to the mind of God, and He stated that He will have mercy on whom He will (Romans 9:15), should we not give God and Him alone the opportunity to judge others in reference to these matters? He knows the inner workings of our hearts and will reward us accordingly. The text seems to have some relevance to the broader principle of stewardship and not to tithing.

> **Acts 4:32-5:11 –**
>
> *"All the believers were one in heart and mind. No one claimed that any of his possessions was his own, but they shared everything. . . .*
>
> *There were no needy persons among them. For from time to time those who owned lands or houses sold them, brought the money from the sales and put it at the apostles' feet, and it was distributed to anyone as he had need.*
>
> *Joseph, a Levite from Cyprus, whom the apostles called Barnabas (which means Son of Encouragement), sold a field he owned and brought the money and put it at the apostles' feet."* (vs. 32, 34-7).

This passage of scripture expresses the reaction of the early Christian converts who were primarily concerned about giving generously, not for a building program, nor to support the disciples, preachers, evangelists and or their ministry, but for the support of the less fortunate or economically deprived – poor members. Many sold their homes and lands and donated the funds to the apostles who in turn distributed them to *". . .every man according as he had need"* (vs.35). Yet this text is linked, if only peripherally, to the tithing law or principle by many preachers.

These early Christian pioneers did not sell their possessions and give a tithe, which they could have done, but sacrificially gave all in consideration of the greater need of the economically impoverished or those who were truly in need. What a marvelous example they established for us but somewhere along our historical path, we have diverted and gone in a completely different direction. How many Christians today would sell their homes and other valuables to create some relief for poor members or to provide some type of financial equality among church members? Too many Christians today think of storing up in their barns and when they become too full, they tear down and build larger ones for greater storage.

Unfortunately, who can blame them for such selfish behavior? Many of them are just reacting to the socio-economic situation in their milieu. When true love and a spirit of generosity are absent, combined with a lack of genuine care in so many churches, the natural thing is to look out for yourself and make sure that your economic future is relatively secured. This type of behavior runs against the grain of or is in contradiction to the principle of unselfishness and should be avoided at all cost, but the reaction involved is understood because when members are in need on many occasions, there is no one available to bear their financial burdens. So those who can, prepare for the days when they can't and are unable to physically work to support themselves. What does this say in reference to the type of loving-caring relationship that should exist in the body of Christ? Don't we long for the day when the ideal will become the reality in God's church?

I saw on the NBC morning show on Monday, July 7, 2008, a White American family of four that was experiencing the American dream (very large and expensive home etc.), had a daughter who spent much of her time in soup kitchens and other places feeding the hungry. The said daughter was able to influence her family to sell its home and downsize by purchasing a smaller one, and donating the sizable profit to the building of schools and the promotion of education in the country of Ghana. When the family who bought their home heard the reason why they sold it, that family donated $100,000.00 to the same cause. I have no idea if these families are Christians, but what they did stand as a monumental example for Christians to follow.

That which is exceptionaly unusual about verse 37 of the above passage is the **Levite** named Barnabas who sold his field and donated all the money to the needy. **Levites** were members of the tribe of Levi who did not give money to their brethren, but received tithe from them for their support. Now one of them who became a Christian did not demand support or a tithe according to the law, but gave all in the interest of a more worthy cause. *Is this scriptural passage a direct or indirect indication of the annulment of the tithing law?* Was this Levite cognizant of the abrogation of his Levitical role with the death of Christ why he did not command or demand a tithe but gave to support the needy? And was he aware that the tithing law was annulled why

104

he did not request a tithe from the brethren? The answer is unknown and the act of this single individual may be insufficient to draw an objective conclusion about the tithing issue, but it seems to peak one's curiosity in reference to this matter.

Other texts that are usually linked to, in order to validate the current teaching and apparent misleading existence of the tithing law are:

Romans 12:13 –

"Share with God's people who are in need. Practice hospitality."

In the more restrictive context of the chapter containing this verse, Paul claims that love is to be sincere and that Christians should be devoted to one another, and honor each other above themselves. In so doing, it becomes difficult to escape sharing with one another or practicing hospitality. In other words, Christians have a social responsibility to relieve the pain and suffering, financially or otherwise, of people in general but more so of those whom they refer to as brethren and sisters. It is very evident that from a contextual perspective, this verse has relevance to the broad concept of stewardship and no bearing to the principle of tithing.

The same is true for the following in **Romans 15: 26, 27** which reads,

"For Macedonia and Achaia were pleased to make a contribution for the poor among the saints in Jerusalem. They were pleased to do it, and indeed

105

they shared in the Jews' spiritual blessings, they owe it to the Jews to share with them their material blessings."

This and other passages written by Paul are clear indications that Paul was on a mission to relieve the suffering of poverty experienced by the Jewish saints in Jerusalem. He did his best to involve as many churches as was possible in the effectuation of this precious mission. It was not just the money that was important to Paul, but the reflection of the love and concern of the Gentile brethren for their Jewish brothers and sisters. Sometimes, I wonder how much knowledge is shared amongst churches in reference to their financial state and especially about the awareness of those small ones that are truly struggling financially as a collective body and as individuals. I am struggling to remember when was the first and or last time I heard of any church recognizing the needs of any other and reaching out to help that church. It is something we are called to do and for the most part, we have "dropped the ball." Too great a concern is placed on other matters and you can assume what those are.

1Corinthians 16:1, 2 –

"Now about the collection for God's people: Do what I told the Galatian churches to do. On the first day of the week, each one of you should set aside a sum of money in keeping with his income, saving it up, so that when I come no collections will have to be made."

As was mentioned earlier, the widespread nature of Christians' involvement in this poverty relief mission for the poor Jerusalem church members is very evident. And it is safe to conclude that this effort by Paul was not related to tithe paying or church offerings as was known then and in the twenty-first century. It was collected for the poor only. It was also an idea for which the members were to plan very carefully. In order to avoid impulsive or hurried giving and be regretful upon realizing that one's contribution exceeded one's means, Paul exhorted the members to set aside thoughtfully their portion on the first day of the week, far in advance of the collection time.

In addition, he instructed them to give in proportion to their income/means. He wanted all to share in the relief, but they were to do so proportionally. And that which is so obvious is the fact that Paul never suggested a percentage, upper or lower limit, as the basis of their giving. This was a freewill offering or contribution. Contextually speaking, this passage(s) has no relevance to tithing or offerings as we know them today, but seems to have some peripheral connection to stewardship. The same conclusion can be justifiably made about 2 Corinthians 8:1-2. Now we move to other provocative passages of scripture.

> **2 Corinthians 8:7, 11-14 –**
>
> *". . .see that you also excel in this grace of giving. . . .*
>
> *Now finish the work, so that your eager willingness to do it may be matched by your completion of it, according to your means.*

> *For if the willingness is there, the gift is acceptable according to what one has, not according to what he does not have.*
>
> *Our desire is not that others might be relieved while you are hard pressed, but that there might be equality.*
>
> *At the present time your plenty will supply what they need, so that in turn their plenty will supply what you need. Then there will be equality."*

In this passage of scripture, Paul is continuing to encourage generosity amongst the Corinthian brethren. He stated in no uncertain terms that their giving should be based on their means or that which were in their possession, not on what they did not have. In other words, do not burden yourselves and use your "credit cards" as a means of contributing unless it is a "debit card" on which account is deposited your personal wealth. Paul did not encourage them to contribute based on a percentage of their income or possession, but allowed them the freedom to be led by the Spirit of God in the determination of their contributions.

Paul's expectation was for them to act or give willingly because in so doing, their gifts would have been acceptable to God. He did not intend for their giving to be a burden in order to relieve those in Jerusalem since such a situation would create and or reverse the problem and set in motion another fundraising to assist them. Paul was attempting to create an equality of means amongst the early Christians and he did not employ the restrictive tithing law or principle, but gave them the opportunity to give out of the generosity of their hearts. These instructions continue to reverberate in the following passages.

2 Corinthians 9: 6-8 (NIV)

"Remember this: Whoever sows sparingly will also reap sparingly, and whoever sows generously will also reap generously.

Each man should give what he has decided in his heart to give, not reluctantly or under compulsion, for God loves a cheerful giver.

For God is able to make all grace abound to you, so that in all things at all times, having all that you need, you will abound in every good work."

It is quite obvious that Paul continues to emphasize the rewards of generous giving. This time, he adds or uses the metaphoric image of the saints freely sowing and reaping as much seeds as they desire. In general, or if all the natural conditions are aligned in favor of the farmer, the more seed he/she plants, the more he/she will reap. But it is the "farmer's" responsibility and freedom to decide the path he/she wants to follow.

Paul encourages the Corinthian saints to determine freely that which they can afford to give from the heart and once that is decided, the offering should be given cheerfully. In other words, their giving should be based on an internal resolve and not from a casual or externally compulsive imposition that may create doubts and a feeling of pressure being exerted upon them that in turn may cause them to think they had no other choice. Under the latter condition, the gift would not be contributed cheerfully and, therefore, unacceptable.

This unacceptability of the gift due to the givers' reluctance would result in the forfeiture of the rewards or blessings. It would have been better if the giver had not even attempted to give. I am convinced also that giving with the idea of being rewarded may be unacceptable. We should give because we love God supremely and our fellowmen dearly, and realize that we have an obligation to contribute to causes that will bring relief to those who are suffering.

I remember so vividly an exceptionally brilliant professor at Michigan State University, the late **Dr. Paul L. Dressel** who employed my wife as his Research Assistant out of many applicants and took a liking to us. He was Professor Emeritus when we came in contact with him and he never professed to be a Christian, but what unprecedented generosity he dished out in large measure to my wife and me. This good-hearted man took us to the faculty lounge for a celebration after successfully passing our comprehensive exams and subsequently volunteered to read our dissertations which he completed in a very short time.

He also prepared us for our dissertation defenses and after being successful, he took us back to the faculty lounge and then to his home where many people were waiting to congratulate us in grand style. At the end of it all, I approach him and asked reluctantly, "Dr. Dressel, how much do we owe you for all the invaluable things you have done for us?" His response was, ***"You owe me nothing, pass it on."*** Years later, I heard Oprah Winphrey encouraging her television audience in a show to "pass it on." Dr. Paul Dressel did not provide assistance to us and probably others with the expectation of receiving a reward. He did so out of a willing and generous heart. Thank God for the exemplary giving of such a man that stands as a monumental stature for all to admire and imitate.

I am convinced that even though the apostle Paul wrote about a reward for giving, he wanted the Corinthians to give out of the love and generosity of their hearts. It was a medium of countering selfishness and avoiding the natural question, "What's in it for me?"

It is very safe to conclude that after a close examination and or contextual analysis of all the passages of scripture mentioned in this chapter, with the exclusion of those in the Synoptic Gospels and Hebrews, they were all addressing the collection of offerings and or the selling of houses and lands to relieve the economic suffering of the poor in the Jerusalem church in order to bring about some semblance of economic equality amongst the brethren. Many of the donors were poor themselves but were delighted to contribute to the needs of their brothers and sisters in Christ. As is clearly evidenced, these N.T. passages have no relationship, connection or relevance to tithing or tithe paying, nor church offerings as we know them in twenty-first century.

Once again, if tithe paying and offerings were "legally" compulsory and spiritually beneficial in the O.T., and relevant in the New Dispensation, why did Paul come so close to writing about the collection of offerings for the poor and never mentioned anything about tithes and offerings for ministers, pastors, evangelists and church support staff etc.. If one's compliance with the tithing law is so critical to one's salvation since the opposite is tantamount to robbing God and one's eternal destruction, why is it that Paul did not state unequivocally and in direct teaching or instruction the importance of tithe paying? And why is it that they preached the gospel and never included in their proclamation the obligation of tithing and offerings for their support and the poor instead of collecting for the poor only.

Paul was not present at the beginning of the early church of Acts 4 when many of the brethren sold their houses and lands and contributed the sums to the Apostles to help those in need, but when he became a converted apostle, he followed in the footsteps of the early Christian converts. Paul's and the other disciples' primary objective was the creation of some sense of equality of means among Christians by taking care of the needs of those who needed economic assistance. Christians making sure that their brothers and sisters did not continue to suffer in their poverty while others lived in luxury. Paul's emphases were preaching the gospel and caring for the needs of poor church members.

However, the following verses **appear** to present a challenge for those who believe in the dissolution of the entire sacrificial system, including the tithing precept, at the cross. Let us examine their true meaning and the author's apparent intention based on some contextual analyses.

1 Corinthians 9:4-14 –

"Don't we have a right to food and drink? Don't we have the right to take a believing wife along with us, as do the other disciples and the Lord's brothers and Cephas? Or is it only I and Barnabas who must work for a living?

Who serves as a soldier at his own expense? Who plants a vineyard and does not eat of its grapes? Who tends a flock and does not drink of the milk? . . .

If we have sown spiritual seed among you, is it too much if we reap a material harvest from you? If others have this right of support from you, shouldn't we have it all the more?

But we did not use this right. On the contrary, we put up with anything rather than hinder the gospel of Christ (1 Cor. 9:4-12, NIV)

The above-mentioned scriptural verses (including 13 and 14 that are quoted later in this section) are the quintessential (most typical or representative) example used by numerous modern-day preachers, pastors, evangelists and ministers etc. as a justification for preaching and teaching about the survival of the tithing law when Christ died on the cross. This is also in harmony with their misguided thought about the transference of the Old Testament economic components of the sacrificial system (tithe/offerings system) and their application to the New Dispensation or Christian era. In addition, they claim entitlement to them, particularly the tithe, based on their self-imposed typological conclusion. So one will ineluctably ask the question, what did Paul mean when he wrote this apparent defense in reference to his freedom in Christ, apostleship, and non-material/limited support from church members as compared to that of his contemporaries – original disciples of Christ – and those who functioned at the altar (Levites and Priests) in the O. T. sacrificial system?

In order to fully comprehend the meaning of these verses devoid of any presupposition or implied instructional revelation for all Christians, it is critically important to spend sufficient time in the performance of some contextual analyses to discover the true rationale for his comparative expressions, because Paul was not just engaged in some philosophical argumentation but appears to be applying sound logics and theological principles in his provision of some solutions to the divisional problems plaguing the Corinthian Church. Without going into too much detail, a few of the problems he addressed in the chapters leading up to chapter 9, were: 1. members taking members to secular courts, 2. conjugal relationships and the culturally immoral influences embraced by some of the brethren, and 3. the consumption of meats offered to idols by some.

It was immediately following his address of the issue concerning the eating of meats offered to idols that Paul mentioned the knowledge or greater understanding possessed by some members in reference to the unreality of idols and the non-sacrilegious nature of meats offered to them as a justification for their consumption of those meats. In spite of that reality and their freedom in Christ to do so, Paul was very concerned about the weak brother, who lacked such knowledge while seeing the stronger engaged in such meat eating activities, may be led astray. Not because the stronger was violating any religious principle or doing anything wrong, but because the weaker lacked the knowledge and may be led astray in his false conclusion that the stronger was being sacrilegious in his action.

In other words, the essence of Paul's response according to William Barclay is that "**Our conduct should always be guided not by the**

thought of our own superior knowledge, but by sympathetic and considerate love for our fellow man. And it may well be that for his sake we must refrain from doing and saying things which we might well do and say" (Letters to the Corinthians, P. 85).

Paul's conclusion on this issue became the launching pad for the analogous comparisons of his freedom and apostleship, and the material support to which he was entitled. He seems to base the latter on those things which his contemporaries were receiving but which he was not. In the final analysis, however, he claimed none of those rights for fear of what some church members thought about his apostleship and how his claim to those rights may affect their perception of him, the messenger, and how this in turn may impact negatively the onward movement of the gospel. This idea was in complete harmony with his conclusion about the effect of the stronger brother's behavior on the weaker brother, even though the stronger was not engaged in the conscious or unconscious contravention of any religious principle (he did nothing wrong by eating meats offered to idols), but to save the weaker due to his lack of knowledge, the stronger refrained from his engagement in that activity.

One cannot but admit, however, that Paul expounded and or articulated an exceptionally brilliant, powerful, impressive, logical and cogent argumentation for his entitlements, but at the exclusion of the contextual association of his presentation on the consumption of meats offered to idols, it does appear as if he was referencing the transference and application of the "financial" aspect of the O.T. sacrificial system to and in, respectively, the Christian Dispensation. But before any definitive conclusion is made, further linguistic analysis of the above-mentioned scriptural passages needs to be undertaken.

There is no doubt that Paul had many critics, some of whom believed that he was not even an apostle (1Cor. 9:1, 2; Gal. 1:1, 15—2:10 etc.). He, however, defended his apostleship and the rights associated with the work of preaching the gospel to the Gentiles on a full-time basis. He mentioned the rights for him and Barnabas to have food to eat and drink, and a wife as the other original apostles (those who were with Jesus) were experiencing. Then he went into this powerfully logical comparison of the fact that a soldier does not pay for his own services; the vineyard keeper partakes of the fruits of the vineyard; the shepherd who cares for the flock drinks of the milk the sheep produce; and "the ox that treaded out the corn" (9:9) by law should not be muzzled but allowed to eat of the corn. Then he logically follows up with the idea that he and those with him were sowing spiritual things and why should they not be entitled to reap some carnal rewards from the Corinthians?

He was a full-time and very devoted evangelist (with others) and, therefore, entitled to food and drink or what he referred to as the *"... right of support from you"* as others enjoy. This seems to give the impression that some of the apostles who were engaged in similar evangelistic activities were definitely receiving material support while he and Barnabas were overlooked or denied similar support. The situation appears to have been, in the mind of Paul, so blatantly discriminatory that he included it in his writing to the Corinthian brethren as a way of bringing it to their attention, but was it for that reason only?

In verse twelve of the said chapter (9:12), Paul claims that if those said apostles have those rights, so should he and Barnabas. Then he made a sudden one-eighty degree turn from his logically powerful argument and writes, *". . .we did not use this right."* Once again, I am brought back to the point of wondering, why even write this when he is cognizant of the irrevocable decision he has made not to accept the same or similar support as did the other disciples. Or was Paul using his refusal of something that was so significant to him as an analogous support of his conclusion about the stronger brother giving up his right to eat meats offered to idols, which was not a sin or contravention of any biblical principle, in order to save the weaker brother. However, in that same verse, he proceeds to provide his rationale for so doing. *"On the contrary, we put up with anything rather than hinder the gospel of Christ"* (1Cor. 9:12, NIV).

It appears that Paul was very aware of the "rights" associated with the grand but challenging mission of taking the gospel message to the Gentiles that he was assigned by our Lord and Savior. On the other hand, he seems to have been ultrasensitive about the issues surrounding his apostleship and the material support to which he was entitled, and the negative consequences on the gospel moving forward that may materialize from the acceptance of his entitlements. He was also very aware of his former role as persecutor of Christians as was stated by him on several occasions, and the paradigm-changing nature of the gospel he received from Jesus.

Preaching this special gospel was a privilege and duty for Paul, and any monetary or other situation that would potentially create any distraction or discredit to the gospel must be avoided at all cost.

The gospel message he had and continued to deliver could not be separated from the messenger. In other words, the messenger had to be a clear and convincing reflection or representation of the message, and he was determined to make sure that there was no contradiction between the message and his deportment. He decided to maintain clean hands. As a result, he was resigned to continue working with his hands (tent making) to support himself and others in ministry.

If this is the case thus far, it is needful to continue the analysis because in the following two verses (13, 14), Paul reverted back to the issue of material support by referencing the functions of the Levites and priests in the temple, and how they were paid for their services even though he did not mention the concepts of tithes and offerings, which were the two means by which they were supported. And once again, it appears that Paul is attempting to make a very significant statement in what appears to be a rhetorical question about how temple functionaries made a living (tithes and offerings), followed by a very convincingly authoritative statement from the Lord as to the source from which preachers should receive their living.

> *"Don't you know that those who work in the temple get their food from the temple, and those who serve at the altar share in what is offered at the altar? In the same way, the Lord has commanded that those who preach the gospel should receive their living from the gospel" (9:13, 14, NIV).*

Was Paul presenting a duality of solutions in the continued defense of the weaker brother since he followed up these verses with a rejection of his material support to which he was entitled? Or was he presenting the idea of tithes and offering transference based on an extrapolation from how the O.T. temple priests and Levites received a living to that of the Christian era and preachers?

It does appear as though he was performing both. Based on the context of the original issue (meats offered to idols), it seems that Paul was continuing the use of his analogous rights and his rejection of them as a support mechanism to demonstrate to the brother(s) who was wrongfully accused of consuming meats offered to idols that, even though he had a right to eat the meats because there was nothing sacrilegious about so doing, it was necessary to give up that right in order to save the weaker brother because of his love and compassion for him.

There is, however, quite a large number of people and preachers who are convinced that Paul's reference to the method of how the temple functionaries were paid for their services and his statement that the Lord commanded those who preach the gospel should live by the gospel, is a clear and convincing statement that modern-day preachers are entitled to a tithe and offerings from God's people. There are some very serious problems associated with this idea and they will be mentioned later in this book.

That which is very fascinating is that Paul cited the spiritual work of temple functionaries and how they were rewarded or paid for what they continued to do in his day, and apparently likened that to how preachers in the New Dispensation should be paid or rewarded. And this time, he added a divine command in this profound statement that God has ordained gospel preachers to live by the gospel. The question is, how can anyone who preaches the gospel live by it? And why did he reject the idea of any reward or compensation for that which he was doing while the other disciples or apostles and preachers were receiving and accepting material support? If this was Paul's conviction, why did he raise or write about these ideas when he had no intention of accepting them? And what did he mean by making a living from the gospel?

In Paul's day, preaching the gospel was not like a modern-day gospel delivery mega business enterprise that made products or generated significantly useful information to sell for a profit, and then use the profit to finance the operation of the business. The gospel dissemination was and still is a service that should not be packaged and sold as a product for profit, and then use that profit to pay the salaries of those preaching it, so what did he really mean?

Before I attempt to present an objective answer(s) to the question, based on my deduction from Paul's writing, let me draw your attention to that which Paul wrote subsequent to his citation of the manner in which the priests and Levites made a living. He reverted back to the rejection of his entitlements again in spite of the idea being a command from the Lord. He wrote in verse fifteen, ***"But I have not used any of these rights. And I am not writing this in hope that you will do such things for me. I would rather die than have anyone deprive me of this boast."*** Then in verses sixteen through eighteen, he writes about his "voluntary compulsion" to preach and his reward for so doing. The reward he mentioned is ***"... Just this: that in preaching***

the gospel I may offer it free of charge, and so not make use of my rights in preaching it" (vs. 18),

Earlier in this section, I mentioned the issue Paul cited in the early part of 1 Cor. 9 concerning the material support given to the other apostles who were engaged in similar or full-time gospel proclamation. There was nothing negative about the issue that he mentioned but seems to have embraced it and even claimed to be entitled to the said support. This material support was not tithe and offerings, which by law, was given exclusively to the O.T. priests and Levites for their work in the temple. It was church members sensing the need to support those involved in full-time evangelistic work and did so voluntarily. So when Paul mentioned how the priests and Levites were paid and claimed a command from the Lord that those who preach the gospel should live by the gospel, what did he mean as I asked before?

Is the implication a direct revelatory instruction from the Lord that ushered in a change in the priestly law that made anyone who chose full-time gospel preaching as a vocation would automatically become genealogically connected to Aaron and his father's family, and gain the right to the tithe and offering? The problems associated with this notion are as follows:

Paul was neither a priest, Levite nor a direct descendent of Aaron or his father, so based on the law of assigned ownership, he had no claim to the tithe and offerings that were assigned by God to the Levites with a tenth of the tithes going to the priests. And he did not mentioned anything in reference to the change of that law or gave any indication that the law had changed, so why the reference as to how the temple functionaries were supported?

As I asked previously, was Paul making an extrapolation for transference of the economic system established by God for the sustenance of the temple workers in the Old Dispensation to that of the New Dispensation? If that was his intention, how would that be ethical or acceptable to God in light of the fact that when the Lamb of God, Jesus Christ, was sacrificed on the cross, the entire sacrificial system was negated and or abrogated? Or are we to believe that Paul was suggesting the survival of the heave, cereal, peace, trespass, wave offerings etc. and the tithe at the cross, while the burn/sin offering was annulled or done away with when He died on that cross?

One thing is very clear and that is, Paul never mentioned the use of the tithe and offering for the support of his or the ministry of others. He was an exceptionally distinguished evangelist and entitled to some kind of support. But was the mention or reference to how the Levites and priests were supported an indirect instruction by implication that the economic support engine of the sacrificial system should be transferred and or implemented in the New Dispensation or Christian era in God's church? Or was he suggesting that some other similar means of support to that of the temple should be implemented in the church for all gospel preachers/workers?

Due to a lack of any direct revelatory instruction in reference to the specific type of support system to be applied for the support of those in full-time gospel preaching in the Christian era, *one can conclude that Paul was comparing and applying a general religious principle of giving material support to those who served in the temple and suggesting something similar, not the same, for those who were and are engaged in full-time gospel preaching.* But is the principle to be interpreted and applied in the same form as was done in the O.T.? Or was he thinking of another method due to the fact that the tithe and offerings were only for the Levites and priests, and that he and the apostles/disciples, including all modern-day preachers, were NOT genealogically connected to the Levitical tribe and had no "legal" right to the tithe?

It appears that Paul was not suggesting the application of the tithing principle, otherwise, this would have been the critically appropriate moment for him to have articulated (written) direct instruction on "paper" as to the validity and applicability of the tithing system in the new Christian era if this was his intention. Paul was very cognizant of the fact that if he had suggested the application of the tithing principle in the Christian Church, he and those who did would have been stoned to death for claiming that which was exclusively for the priests or Levites. Should it be assumed, therefore, that the idea of a new financial support system was there in his head/mind but the details were not yet developed? Or was Paul thinking about the collection of an offering for the support of the ministry as was done for the poor? This is extremely unsettling due to a lack of a definitively direct statement from Paul on this issue or subject matter.

If Paul's intention was to seek a specific system of financial support for those involved in preaching the gospel on a full-time basis, why would he have mentioned in verse eighteen (1Cor. 9:18) his selective preference to offer it "free of charge" and deny himself the rights associated with this mission? He seems to have embraced or accepted the material support given to the other apostles and did not advise them to refuse it. However, it is important to bear in mind that the support they received was neither the tithe nor the offering intended for the priests and Levites, a system that still was in existence in Paul's day but not accepted by Christians subsequent to the death of Christ on the cross. The said support was funds voluntarily given by individual church members for the partial and or full sustenance of those disciples involved in full-time evangelistic work.

It is almost absolutely safe to definitively conclude that there is no evidence of a linguistic nature to claim that Paul advocated, in 1Cor. 9, the transference and application of the tithing law from the O.T. to the Christian Dispensation. If he did, why would he agree and even write about the sustained material support given to his contemporaries. It would not be congruent or in harmony with the tithing law for those Christians to voluntarily decide the amount to be given when the law has already specified the amount to be given.

In addition, the material contributions made to the apostles provided for their needs and somewhat restricted them from being involved in gospel peddling that Paul was highly against. In 2 Corinthians 2:17 (NIV), he wrote about those who corrupt the word of God as follows; *"Unlike so many, we do not peddle the word of God for profit. On the contrary, in Christ we speak before God with sincerity, like men sent from God."* The said scriptural passage in the Amplified Bible reads,

> *"For we are not, like so many, [like hucksters making a trade of] peddling God's Word [short-changing and adulterating the divine message]; but like [men] of sincerity and the purest motive,*

as [commissioned and sent] by God, we speak [His message] in Christ (the Messiah), in the [very] sight and presence of God" **(2 Cor. 2:17, AB).**

What is the meaning of the words "corrupt" and "peddling" as are used in both versions and their importance to the subject matter at hand? The Greek word used is "kapeleuso" (the accents are omitted) which comes from the word "kapelos" for a retailer, huckster, a profiteer or one who does something for personal profit. The idea is to use the Word of God to preach and or teach for personal gain. In other words, "It means to profiteer from God's Word, to preach for money or to profess faith for personal gain" (Spiros Zodhiates, **The Complete Word Study Dictionar**y, N.T., p. 819).

A similar notion is also mentioned in the book of 2Peter 2:3. It is a description of those, who in their pernicious ways, will act as gospel merchants in their attempts to deceive God's people through the use of *". . .feigned words make merchandise of you . . ."* (2 Pet. 2:3, KJV). This appears to be a deliberate act of such people who extract money from Christians in exchange for their gospel deception which would also be a type of gospel peddling.

So when we think of what Jesus did with His disciples by sending them out to preach the gospel and heal the sick etc. without any money or change of clothing, was He attempting to inform them and future disciples or gospel workers to depend on Him for their every need, and expect no monetary gain in exchange for their work? Peter understood the concept because he was one of the disciples sent out without anything, but how was Paul informed or made cognizant of the words of Jesus in reference to this idea that motivated him to warn those of his day, as well as potential gospel preachers and or teachers, to avoid gospel peddling.

If those engaged in gospel dissemination, full- or part-time, are not to preach or teach for monetary gain, should they also go in raw faith with the understanding that Jesus, through people, will take care of their material needs? Jesus did not instruct His disciples, past, present and future, to collect a tithe and or offering for their support, but to go in faith and depend on the benevolence of those whom He will direct to care for them. This is exactly what the disciples did during and subsequent to the Day of Pentecost. They did not charge, nor did they collect any funds in exchange for preaching the gospel but were cared for by many who understood the importance of financially supporting those who were engaged in full-time evangelistic preaching and or teaching.

I can only assume that based on Jesus' knowledge of the diabolic corruption that took place in the O.T. priestly system over the many years of its existence, He would not have endorsed the collection of the tithe for the continuation of the similar system, not even to pay or as a reward for modern-day gospel workers, for fear of a repetition of the said corruption. Generic man's nature has not changed over time and given the opportunity for the spirit of greed to be awakened in modern preachers, due to the differentiation in the structural distribution of pay or wages (tithe) for gospel disseminators etc., this would not be a good idea.

And as we are very aware, that which is currently paid to some twenty-first century preachers from the unauthorized collection of

126

tithes from their brethren appears to be insufficient to care for the needs of such people and their families. So many are engaged in other lines of work, including the further peddling of the gospel in other churches to make up the difference needed to "sufficiently" care for the economic needs or wants of their families. The exceptions are the multi-million dollar televangelists.

It is no surprise that Paul included as one of the criteria for eldership or the spiritual leadership of God's church that such leaders should not be "*. . .given to filthy lucre*" (Titus 1:7, KJV; check 1Peter 5:2). It is a warning for shepherd-servant leaders against greed and how that diabolical spirit can lead one to making money by any means possible. Christians and their leaders are to be so well disciplined that they adjust their needs to suit their means and are not compelled to increase their means to meet their needs. When that discipline to adjust one's needs is absent, the possibility of being tempted to engage in things that are unethical is ever present and can lead to one's ruin. There are numerous examples in life of those who chose to go down that path.

Going back to Christ's selected method of members' or other people's benevolence for the support of gospel workers in His day, do you think that He is expecting anything more or less of us today? However, the modern-day institutionalization of the gospel and professionalization of the ministry by man have changed the whole dynamics of the church in reference to gospel delivery, and Christ's method appears to be an insufficient means to care for the needs of all gospel professionals in modernity. Is this the reason why some denominations have selected to reinstate that which was annulled at the cross, the tithe and offerings system? If this is the case, they need to justify their tithing reinstatement with scripture to prove its validity in the Christian era. Unfortunately, it appears that since the death of Christ, there is no N.T. scriptural passage that can be used as objective evidence in support of the tithing reinstatement. This should create within all of us the desire to reexamine the current status of financing the gospel proclamation to discover its alignment with the word of God.

In spite of what has been stated above, there are proponents who argue from a typological perspective that N.T. ministers, preachers, and or pastors are a type of O.T. priests and entitled to the tithe. If this is the case, then why did the Apostle Peter write that God's people are *". . . an holy priesthood, to offer up spiritual sacrifices, acceptable to God by Jesus Christ"* in 1Peter 2:5? In the New Dispensation, God's people do not need the services of human priests any more since they are all priests and have direct access to their High Priest, Jesus Christ our Lord. It is His priestly intermediary service that all "clergy" and "Laity" need.

Let us return to the above-mentioned argument of ministers being a type O.T. priest and entitled to the tithe. As was stated earlier, the tithe was given by God to the Levites as a reward for their work in the Sanctuary and they in turn paid a tenth to the priests. In other words, the Levites, who were not priests and could not become priests based on the law, received ninety percent of the collected tithes as a reward for their services in the said Sanctuary that later became the Temple. They kept it clean; prepared supplies such as oils and incense, music etc. for the smooth and effective operation of the temple worship services. Therefore, if Paul was suggesting a similar economic support structure to be applied to the church in the Christian era, there would be a great number of people who would be eligible (elders, deacons, superintendents etc.) to receive support or be paid on a part- or full-time basis for the work they do in the Christian church.

Another scriptural passage that is generally cited in support of ministers/pastors claiming their right to the tithe as a payment for what they do, is 1Timothy 5:18 which states, *". . . For the scripture saith, Thou shalt not muzzle the ox that treadeth out the corn. And, The labourer is worthy of his reward."* This text was cited previously in the discussion of 1Cor. 9. Nothing of an extensive nature was written about it but in this context, at least two things are worthy of address in this passage.

The first is that Paul was writing about the spiritual shepherd-servant leaders or Elders (not pastors) who deserved to be honored, especially those who work hard in the body of Christ. This scriptural reference has nothing to do with tithing since they, the Elders, were not descendants of Levi and by law were not entitled to the collection of tithe from the people.

The second is that it refers to a proverbial saying that was quoted by Jesus in Luke 10: 7 which is based on an O.T. law that an ox must not be muzzled while threshing the corn. This would allow the ox to eat as much of the corn as it needed for energy replenishment that may be considered as a reward for its work. Just as the ox was entitled to a reward for its work, Paul was suggesting that a laborer has a right to his/her reward, irrespective of who that person may be, and including the church Elder. However, Paul did not state the type of reward to which he or they was/were entitled respectively.

In addition, we are all priests and ministers of the gospel. The gospel commission was not given to pastors and or evangelists only, but to all people who accept Jesus as their Lord and Savior. They all have a spiritual responsibility to voluntarily make the love of God known to a dying world and what Christ has done for the entire human family without any financial reward. So all have a role to play in teaching, preaching, caring, counseling etc., and this represents a greater portion of the work than that which is performed by preachers and or pastors, and this group of people is referred to as the "laity" which is a non-biblical term and used to divide God's people into two major classes with the "clergy" being perceived as the "superior" class due to the ordination and setting aside for professional ministry.

Paul must be congratulated for the position he took in not pursuing the "fight" for support from the church and the rationale for his decision is understandable. However, one is left to wonder why Paul made himself the exemplary exception in this matter by not accepting church members' financial support as the major means of his sustenance, but by working with his hands to support himself in tent making while preaching the gospel on a full-time basis. Did he ever think about how that example would affect future debates on this support issue? There are times when I think that Paul did not even realize how powerful and influential a figure he would have become and how significance his writings would have been to the Christian Church.

If Paul was suggesting the implementation of the tithing law in the New Dispensation, how would his statements in Hebrews 7 and 8, Ephesians 2 and Colossians 2 harmonize with this idea? There is one seismic event that shook up and dismantled the whole sacrificial system that will provide some clarification on the issue. **The death of Christ on the cross changed everything in reference to the entire sacrificial system and all related ceremonial laws, including the tithe and offerings**. It discarded the old and replaced it with a totally new system. Let us examine the critical changes that occurred upon His death and return later to the importance of material support for full-time gospel workers.

The Death of Christ Changed Everything

When Christ *"...cried out again in a loud voice, he gave up his spirit. At that moment the curtain of the temple was torn in two from top to bottom. . ."* (Matthew 27: 50, 51, NIV). It was at that saddest and exceptionally grief-stricken, yet most significant moment in human history when the Son of God, the sacrificial Lamb of God, gave up the ghost (died) in human form as a result of His crucifixion on that infamous cross and created His separation from the Father that the indispensably durable curtain between the Holy Place and Most Holy Place in the Temple was no match for divine power. It was torn into two parts from top to bottom. But what does this incident mean? What is its theological significance in reference to the change/abrogation and replacement of the whole sacrificial system in the New Dispensation or Christian church era?

It is generally agreed by biblical scholars that the renting of the temple's inner curtain that separated the Holy Place from the Most Holy Place, through which only the High Priest entered once per year (Day of Atonement) to atone for the sin of Israel in the presence of

God, signaled the end or complete annulment of the whole sacrificial system, making it possible for believers to go directly in the presence of God through Jesus Christ our Lord and Savior, our High Priest.

That which is so important to my curiously hungry mind/thought is, what occurred between the time of Christ's death (time spent in the grave) and resurrection, and His first (John 20:17) and second (Acts 1:9) ascension in reference to the atonement for the sin of the human race as our High Priest before the Father? In other words, animal sacrifices were no longer acceptable because He became our atoning sacrifice, but there was no High Priest to plead our case to the Father during that time gap until He ascended and took His rightful place as our High Priest in the heavenly sanctuary. It may be somewhat frivolous to even think of this question, but was the atoning sacrifice on the cross sufficient to cover for us even in His High Priestly functional absence and even if there was (were) a possibility to prevent Him from returning to heaven for whatever reason one can think about? I may never know the answer this side of eternity but I plan to get there and if I remember, the question will be asked. We can rest assured that a situation of this nature was fully taken care of by our omniscient God.

The renting of the Temple curtain must have been something of a traumatically mysterious experience and or event for the priests when one understands the share sizes of those curtains and the exposure of the Most Holy Place where God's presence resided and no one died as a result. According to Alfred Edersheim, ***"The Veils before the Most Holy Place were 40 cubits (60 feet) long and 20 (30 feet) wide, of the thickness of the palm of the hand, and"*** he continues to state that they were ***"wrought in 72 squares which were joined together"*** and *"in the exaggerated language of the time, it took about three hun-dred priests to manipulate each veil"* due to its weight (Edersheim 1974, p.611.

Edersheim also stated that the time of the renting of the veil appears to have coincided with the Evening Sacrifice when the officiating priests entered the holy Place to perform certain sacred rituals or services. To their surprise, they saw for the first time in the history of the sanctuary/temple, the veil torn from top to bottom and *". . .hanging in two parts from its fastenings above at the sides"*, with the priests being able to see through the Most Holy Place where God's presence resided and they were not fatally struck down. This *". . . was indeed, a terrible portent, which would soon become generally known, and must in some form or other, have been preserved on tradition"* (Ibid. pp. 611-12).

The critical question here at hand is, what did the renting of the veil mean to the sacrificial system in part or in whole, and to the continued existence of priests, their functions/roles as mediators and serving at the altar, and any other sub-system instituted for its social and economic support apart from which it could not operate effectively and even remain in existence?

Paul, in **Colossians 2:14,** wrote about the cancellation of *". . .the written code with its regulations, that was against us and that stood opposed to us; he took it away nailing it to the cross."* There are some who believe that the **regulations** stated in this text are the Mosaic laws which would be inclusive of the Ten Commandments. If, however, this moral law was nailed to the cross, then there would be no schoolmaster to lead us to Christ (Galatians 3:24) and where there is no law there is no sin (Romans 7:7, 8). It appears that from a moral/ ethical perspective, the nailing of the Ten Commandments would be socially and spiritually detrimental to both Christians and the general society. It would include the elimination of some very sacred and foundational principles necessary for our guidance through life to our eternal destination by the grace of God. So what are those regulations that were cancelled at the cross?

Paul mentioned a similar idea in Ephesians 2:14, 15 in which he wrote, *"For he himself is our peace, who has destroyed the barrier, the dividing wall of hostility, by abolishing in his flesh the law with its commandments and regulations. His purpose was to create in himself one new man out of the two, thus making peace..."*

It is quite clear that Paul was referring to that divisive wall of hostility that existed between the Jews and Gentiles, and how the death of Christ broke down that social and spiritual wall, and made both groups, Jews and Gentiles, one in Christ. Therefore, the abolition of the "law" with its commandments and regulations once again has nothing to do with the ten commandments as was also confirmed by Jesus who said in Matthew 5:17 that He did not come *"...to abolish the Law or the Prophets; I have not come to abolish them but to fulfill them."* So what commandments and regulations is Paul writing about in these verses? For a more in depth explanation of what was nailed to the cross, let us turn to the book of Hebrews.

In **Hebrews chapter 7:11, 12, 16, 18 and 28**, Paul wrote:

"If perfection could have been attained through the Levitical priesthood (for on the basis of it the law

was given to the people), why was there still need for another priest to come – one in the order of Melchizedek, not in the order of Aaron? (vs. 11)

"For where there is a change of the priesthood, there must also be a change of the law." (vs. 12)

"One who has become a priest not on the basis of a regulation as to his ancestry but on the basis of the power of an indestructible life" (vs. 16).

The former regulation is set aside because it was weak and useless" (vs. 18) and

"For the law appoints as high priests men who are weak; but the oath, which came after the law, appointed the Son, who has been made perfect forever" (vs. 28).

It is apparent that during the life of Christ on earth and before His death on the cross, the temple stood in Jerusalem with the priests functioning as they did for centuries in the offering of animal (sin) sacrifices etc. and the people presenting their tithes and offerings as were commanded in the ceremonial laws, including the Old Testament ecclesiastical, sacrificial, priestly and tithing laws. Unfortunately, nothing of substance is recorded about Christ's participation in both the sacrificial offerings and tithe paying. The former is clearly understood since He knew no sin and was the true Sin Offering, the sacrificial Lamb of God.

But why is there no biblical (N.T.) evidence of Him paying tithe? It can be assumed that, maybe, He did and maybe He did not since everything was not recorded. A close examination of the above quoted passages may provide some indication as to why He did or did not, as was revealed by Paul.

The New Covenant did not take effect while Christ was alive. It did (was ratified) when His blood was shed and His life was sacrificed, and restored after His resurrection upon His ascension into Heaven as our High Priest (Hebrews 4:14, 15; 8:1). After His resurrection etc., Christ became our High Priest and the priesthood status God wanted for Israel that they forfeited due to their disobedience, was bestowed on all Christians according to 1Peter 2:9. This life-sacrificing act of Christ on the cross brought several things to an end, including:

1. the role of the Aaronic priesthood and all other functions/ roles associated with that position,
2. the Levitical (Tribe of Levi) assistants' role,
3. animal sacrifices,
4. the financial system or tithe and offerings, and
5. the entire system of worship. The end of these ushered in the new covenantal dispensation.

The annulment of the above brought into existence the New Covenant which is **kainos** in nature according to Paul. This means that it is not a continuation of nor an added change to the old covenant. It is new in point of time and different in point of quality. And a completely new structure and form of worship had to be instituted to harmonize with the New Covenant. Paul also used the word **gerasko** which means "to become old"; **aphanismos** meaning "to vanish away to destroy" and **palaioo** which means "to render obsolete" (Zodhiates, Spiros, The Complete Word Study Dictionary, N.T., 1993). This means that the New Covenant instituted by Jesus is of a quality that is completely different to and obliterates or cancels the old, which logically includes the economic system instituted to support its operation.

Why would one build an organization with a special financial system for its operation, destroy that organization and allow the underpinning financial system to remain and be applied to a new system without specific instructions as to its relevance and application to the new. Difficult to imagine and comprehend that the tithes and offerings which were set aside by law for the Levites and priests only, were suddenly transferred by the death of Christ on the cross and assigned to the new all-member priests in the Christian era without a specific change of the law or any new instructive information as to the change. How would such a system work unless all are allowed to work and pay tithes and share in both the tithe and responsibilities of caring for the church, as well as communicating the gospel to the ends of the world.

There are some people and organizations who and that respectively believe the death of Christ resulted in the abrogation of the Levitical assistants and Aaronic priesthood, and the sacrificial system exclusive of the tithing law. In other words, the ceremonial laws regulating the sacrificial sin offerings which symbolized Christ atoning sacrifice came to an end but not the tithing law. This they claim, finds support in Jesus' endorsement of tithing in Matthew 23:23. It could also be assumed, as was stated earlier, that Jesus endorsed the priesthood and ceremonial laws when He ordered the healed leper, in Luke

5:12-15 to *". . .go, show thyself to the priest and offer the sacrifice that Moses commanded for your cleansing, as a testimony to them"* **(vs. 14, NIV).** Jesus was correct on both occasions due to the fact that the sacrificial laws were still in existence. **Everything changed when He died on the cross.**

If it is correct that the tithing law was instituted or introduced/ implemented in the sacrificial system to support the Levites and Aaronic priests in their full-time duties at the temple because they had no other inheritance in Israel, would there be of necessity a change of that law that brought about the demise of the priesthood and Levitical helpers, and the introduction of a completely different priesthood of believers who are all expected to function in some capacity for the realization of the gospel commission? In this case, it would be virtually impossible to compensate all for their role in the church.

In addition, **only the Levites and the Aaronic priests and their descendents could receive tithe and offerings from the people. That was the law.** So unless the law was changed or modified to include a selective few who have chosen and were given the oppor- tunity to serve on a full-time basis in ministry, they could not receive tithe and offerings from the people, and there is no indication or evidence of such a change or modification of the law to give the tithe to a select few as was mentioned previously. It does appear that it was and it was abolished with the ceremonial laws.

Paul made it exceptionally clear in Hebrews 7:12 that when there is a change in the priesthood there is also a change in the law. This priesthood change is verified by Peter who refers to God's people in the new Christian era as *". . . like living stones, are being built into a spiritual house to be a holy priesthood offering spiritual sacrifices acceptable to God"* (1Peter 2:5, NIV), and the same (people) are described by him as *". . . a chosen people, a royal priesthood, a holy nation, a people belonging to God . . . ."* (vs.9). In other words, just as God wanted Israel to be a nation of priests (Exodus 19:6), Christ wants the whole body of believers to be priests in the sense that they are to reflect the holiness of their High Priest, Jesus Christ, and have direct access to the Father through that same Mediator.

Let us get back to what Paul really meant by a change of the priest-hood and the ineluctable change of the law or the setting aside of the "former regulations" etc. It logically follows that if the priesthood was initiated with a law that provided all the regulatory instructions/ information about its nature, family restriction, scope of function etc., and that the priesthood was made obsolete by Christ's death, so would the law because it would be "illegal" to receive tithes if that status was changed or made null and void. And the institution of a new priesthood would require a new law.

However, the law and regulations mentioned by Paul refer to the ceremonial laws that regulated every aspect of the sanctuary worship services. All those religious practices were only shadows and symbols pointing to the real sacrificial Lamb of God. Therefore, the death of Christ and the renting of the temple veil signaled the change of the earthly priesthood which was included in that law. The said priesthood became obsolete or null and void because they were only symbols and shadows pointing to the coming of Jesus Christ, the sacrificial Lamb of God. His appearance and successful mission effectuation on the cross created the conditions for a completely radical change that eliminated all the symbols and shadows.

It logically follows that if the Levites were chosen to assist the priests and the priesthood was annulled or made null and void (the priests who were the primary sanctuary figures in the sacrificial system, and their status, roles and functions were no longer valid and spiritually meaningful), there would be no need for the Levites or assistants. This means that there had to be a change in the law of the Levites, although Paul did not directly mention it, in reference to their selection, status and function, and the receiving of tithe from the people.

Let us bear in mind that God selected them (the Levites) to assist the priests in the sacrificial services to ascertain its effective operation. Therefore, if the law of the priesthood was made obsolete and priests were no longer needed to offer mediatory sacrifices, it clearly follows that there was no need for Levites who were commanded to collect tithes from the people and offered or shared ten percent with the priests as a wave offering. **No priests no Levites, and no priests and Levites, no need for tithe and offerings.** They were the only ones, through God's command, in Israel who were allowed to collect tithe and offerings from the people. With the collapse of the entire system of worship came the annulment and obsolescence of the tithing and offering principle as was commanded in the Old Testament.

It would be very similar to a large modern organization with a CEO and many assistants to help him/her fulfill the mission of the company. If the CEO is fired, it does not mean that the assistants would be fired also, but if the company or organization is dissolved through some injunction of the owner(s), or a major product change that forces the company to close its doors and relieve the CEO of his/her duties, it necessarily follows that the assistants would no longer be needed. If the owners decide to develop a new business or organization with a different mission and product line, this would require workers with different knowledge and skills to meet the needs of the new company. You get the idea.

The death of Christ brought about very radical changes. It vanquished the old ceremonial laws inclusive of the sacrificial system – sanctuary, priestly, Levitical, tithing and offering laws. It made the whole system useless and it becomes very difficult to comprehend the survival of the tithing law, with its restrictions in such a revolutionary or paradigmatic change.

Let us assume for argument sake that it did not, how do we figure out who should pay tithe and to whom? Based on the genealogical mandates for the receiving of tithes, how could the church figure out, from a biblical perspective, those individuals who should be considered worthy of such an honor? One would have to go through the very expensive process of discovering the DNA of the Levites and Aaronic priests, and then run tests on those who think that they are linked by genes to either one before an objective decision could be made as was mandated by the law if it is still in existence.

Fortunately, such a procedure is off the table and very unnecessary due to the fact that all believers are priests, according to Peter, which indicates that no one of us is entitled to tithe from any of us. This is not to suggest that the work of God on earth assigned to and done through

His church does not need financial support because it does, something that will be addressed later in this book.

It is very theologically safe to conclude that the death of Christ vanquished the whole sacrificial institution of worship and no component survived the abrogation. It was rendered obsolete. There was no transference or carryover of any sacrificial component from the old to the new because the new covenant is **Kainos,** and it is not a continuation of the old nor something added or subtracted from it. It is new in quality and form. Christ's death introduced a completely different "sanctuary" or church with totally new components.

The New Testament church or the **ekklesia** is not a building structure but the people of God or the body of Christ coming together to worship Him and this can be accomplished in or outside a building facility. "Where two or three are gathered, there I am to bless" (Matthew 18:20). In His body, there are no selective priests since all are priests and He is our only High Priest. If this is the case, tithe and offerings are irrelevant, non-mandatory, "illegal" in such a system. God's presence in the Most Holy Place of the old sanctuary now resides, not in a building, but in the "hearts" of each of His disciples or followers.

In addition, the New Dispensational mission is different to that of the O.T. and requires all believers, including leaders, evangelists, ministers and other members of the ekklesia to fulfill that gigantic mission of the gospel to all the world. Unfortunately, those who are ordained and assigned to proclaim the gospel on a full-time basis are engaged in other line of work as well as functioning as 'CEOs" and preaching to the "choir" on a weekly basis. And an insufficient number of church members is involved in the commission effectuation which means that those who are leading through their sacrificial efforts on a full-time basis (missionaries) should be supported by the body of Christ, but not with a mandated tithe. It should be based on that which each has and not on what each does not have. Nor should those who are economically deprived and can barely scratch out a living for themselves and families be pressured by spiritual guilt and or intimidation to sacrifice their families. Let the Spirit of God lead them in this direction.

Based on the aforementioned, it is also safe to write that the apparent dependence exercised by so many Christian disciples on their "priests", cardinals, pastors and or ministers is one of complete futility if we are all priests or brothers and sisters in Christ, bearing one another's burdens and providing the encouragement we need to stay the course to eternity. We are not a hierarchy of believers with rulers and the ruled/subjects, leaders and dumb sheep or followers, but humble people and leaders who are ready and willing to sacrifice their own good and rights in the best interest of each other. All believers are to be disciples functioning in ministry for the making of other disciples for Jesus according to His commission.

As was mentioned previously, when Jesus said to His disciples *"... go and make disciples of all nations, baptizing them in the name of the Father and of the Son and of the Holy Spirit, and teaching them to obey everything I have commanded you. . ."* **(Matthew 28:19, 20, NIV),** He was also addressing future disciples or those who would accept Him as their Master and Lord through the ages. If we are not engaged, as modern Christian disciples, in the fulfillment of the gospel commission, are we truly disciples of Christ or are we just church members?

Some may think there is no distinction between both groups, but there is. Disciples are church members but church members are not necessarily disciples. Disciples do not attend church services on a regular or irregular basis, sit, listen and then leave in order to return the following week day for more. Disciples listen to the small inner voice of the Holy Spirit, adhere to the teachings of their Master and follow in His footsteps by being involved with those in the church as well as those in their communities with the goal in mind of leading community members to Jesus.

In addition, disciples in the community of Christ (His Church) are all one in Him. All those who have accepted Him through faith and are baptized in Him are to be united with one another and their High Priest, Jesus Christ our Lord and Savior. In other words, Christ through His atoning death on the cross has removed that wall of partition that divided Jews and Gentiles (Ephesians 2:15), and the sin that separated all from God, and has reconciled us to Him and one another. Now *"There is neither Jew nor Greek, slave nor free, male nor female, for you are all one in Christ Jesus"* (Galatians 3:26-8)

Now that all Christians/disciples are hopefully well integrated and equal before God in His body, His church, and it has become virtually impossible to identify those who are and are not genealogically connected to the Levites and Aaronic priests who were the only ones permitted to receive tithe and offerings by a vanquished law, to whom should we pay tithe and offerings? If we give or present tithes and offerings to any other since Christ died on the cross through the twenty-first century, are we not in compliance with an annulled or outdated law that has no relevance in the Christian era?

It is not my intention to "beat a dead horse" but it is critical to mention again that not even when the churches were instructed to give a freewill offering to help the poor in the Jerusalem church (1 Cor. 16:1, 23 etc.), did Paul give any indication, direct or indirect instruction and or encouragement for the brethren to be faithful in returning their tithes and offerings as is done in so many twenty-first century Christian churches. This would have been a critical and or opportune time to do so, but he never did and I wonder why? Was he cognizant at that point in time, subsequent to his Damascus experience, that the death of Christ shattered forever the sacrificial system inclusive of the tithing law? A safe assumption can be made due to his experience of establishing house churches on his first missionary journey without any instruction to those church leaders/members as to the then current validity of that law.

Another critically opportune time occurred in Acts 15 when Paul and Barnabas were returning from their first missionary journey and spent some time with the church of Antioch. They encountered some men of the sect of the Pharisees from Judea who were teaching the Antioch brethren that except they were circumcised and adhered to the laws of Moses, they were destined for exclusion from the salvation offered through the death of Christ on the cross. So after Paul and Barnabas had ". . . no small dissension and disputation with them . . ." (Acts 15:2), the issue was referred to the church of Jerusalem, where a resolution was finally determined by the whole church, including the Apostles and Elders.

This exceptionally wise and Holy Ghost-driven decision was written and sent with representatives from the Jerusalem Church to be delivered in spoken words and letter form to the Antioch brethren. The decision may be considered to be the first codified set of church membership criteria for Christians in addition to their acceptance of Jesus Christ by faith as their Lord and Savior, and their baptism into His. The criteria were designed and intended to be simplistic in nature and non-burdensome to the brethren as is clearly seen in the following:

> *For it seemed good to the Holy Ghost, and to us, to lay upon you no greater burden than these necessary things;*
>
> *That ye abstain from meats offered to idols, and from blood, and from things strangled, and from fornication: from which if ye keep yourselves ye shall do well. Fare ye well* (Acts 1 5:28-9, KJV).

That which is so fascinating about the preamble (vs. 28) and "member criteria" are:

1. The influence of Peter and James in their presentations to the church on the issue as they were moved by the Holy Ghost and their referral to the apparent approval of the Spirit of God on their decision;

146

2. The limited number and simplicity of the criteria as compared with the numerous and complicated twenty-first century membership criteria of many Christian churches; and

3. The descriptive term used to describe and or indicate the significance of the codified moral and ethical standards to which the members were to adhere in their Christian experience. The term is "necessary things" and an appropriate substitute is "indispensable things."

If these are the genuinely paramount standards, revealed by the Holy Spirit to the Christian Church, to which Christians should adhere, why the exclusion of the tithing law and its implementation in the lives of the Jerusalem, Antioch and other Gentiles church members? Why did it take so long, over eighteen hundred years, before the antiquated tithing law was introduced into the Christian community by one of the many Protestant churches? And why was the tithing law/concept rejected for implementation in the Roman Catholic Church over the centuries of its existence while many of the other Protestant churches have accepted it as valid? What biblical proof do they possess that is lacking in the former? Even when Paul discussed the issue of law keeping, he gave no indication and or instruction for Christians to adhere to the tithing law.

The simplicity of the criteria presented to the members of the Antioch Church is that for which numerous Christians are deeply and earnestly seeking – a return to the New Testament model of church and standards. However, another significant aspect of the above-mentioned indispensable criteria, as was briefly mentioned above, is the absence of any financial instruction or obligation to return a faithful tithe and offering to God. Here was the early Christian Church that was not geographically far removed from the center of Judaism in Jerusalem and its on-going ritualistic obligations of animal sacrifices, tithing paying and offering contributions, and there was no instruction from the Apostles and Elders of the Jerusalem Church to include in the church membership criteria for the Antioch and other Christian churches to return tithes and offerings to God through His church. Was it that the church, including the Apostles and Elders, was made aware by the Spirit of God that tithing and all the special offerings were a part of the sacrificial laws that were annulled when Christ died on the cross why they were not included as one of the "necessary" church membership criteria??

This was an era when the church and its leaders, unlike the twenty-first century churches, were exceptionally dependent on the Spirit of God Who appeared to have responded very positively to and through the early church. It was a time of great spiritual awakening, inspiration and revelation from the Spirit, and if there was a carryover of the tithing law from the Old Dispensation to the New, in regards to the significance of this indispensable requirement for church membership, this was certainly the opportune time for such a revelation and it did not occur or happen. So neither the Jerusalem Church nor the newly established Gentiles churches acknowledged the transfer and instructed their members to implement the tithing system in the Christian era or Dispensation.

Fortunately or unfortunately, there are neither direct nor indirect spiritual instructions given to the N.T. Church to be handed down through the ages to Christians regarding the continuation of tithe giving and the restructured distribution of the tithe and offerings. If there were direct teachings in reference to a restructured distribution of the same (tithes and offerings), would this not be problematic for the church in that those classified as the only ones authorized to receive and use/spend tithe and offerings would appear as having a different status and therefore a privileged group among God's people? This would definitively create a deep social/spiritual schism, one type of "wall" Christ died to eradicate from, and one that is potentially harmful to His church. Sometimes, I wonder about the "wall" that was created through the human division of God's church into the two broad categories of clergy and laity, and whether the time will ever come when both groups will begin to perceive themselves as one and equal in Christ?

Fortunately, the above-mentioned current division of clergy and laity in Christianity has no biblical basis for its existence because we are all priests and Christ is our High Priest, yet it exists. There are other divisional categories of office holders and members who are considered to be high class status based on economics (those who contribute significant amounts of money to the church), education and talents/ abilities that are deemed relevant to and applicable for the advancement of the church. While there are the lowly and relatively poor (they lack the ability to contribute significant funds to the church) with gifts that may be perceived as unimportant to the church. There is no doubt that the former is being perceived as more important and treated with greater honor and respect. And there is no doubt that those high class members who contribute lavishly in tithes and offerings are so much more well respected than those who cannot. Let us not forget that the poor and or lowly can sense discriminatory decisions and see the actions taken by leaders and others in favor of the rich and gifted which is partiality and unacceptable in the sight of God. Let us remember that the woman who threw in her last mite, not a tithe of the mite, in the treasury of the Temple was considered to have given more than those who gave out of the abundance of their riches.

All Christians should bear in mind that the Holy Spirit has given diverse gifts to members of the church according to Paul in Romans 12:4-8; 1Corinthians 12:1-31 and Ephesians 4:11, 12 for the sole purpose of preparing *". . . God's people for works of service, so that the body of Christ may be built up until we all reach unity in the faith and in the knowledge of the Son of God and become mature. . . ."* (Ephesians 4:12, 13, NIV). The gifts are not given for God's people to hold offices and do nothing but to cooperatively function (do things) for the edification of His church. The gifts are not given for the inflation of ones' egos or the acquisition of power and authority in His church, but to be used in humility for the internal and external advancement of the work of God on earth.

Fortunately or unfortunately, gifts are not given in the same measure or proportion to every one. Some have one gift and others have many, and the usual reaction of normal human beings is to give greater honor to those with multi talents while "dishonoring" those with one or less. But Paul's advice is to give greater honor to those with the gifts that are considered least of all which is just the opposite of what is normally done in God's church. Remember as I mentioned previously, gifts and talents are given/bestowed on all for the performance of certain or specific functions or roles and not for the holding of offices with or without prestige, and or for self aggrandizement.

In regards to the church, Paul has made a very unique reference to one group of people, and to be more specific, the Ephesian elders, in his farewell speech from Miletus and referred to them as the ones whom the Holy Spirit has made **overseers** of that church (and by implication the Spirit has also ordained the other N.T. elders) and cautioned them to *"Be shepherds of the church of God, which he bought with his own blood. . ."* (Acts 20:28, NIV. See also 1Peter 5:2-4). He further provided additional information to them as to how they should function as **elders or shepherd-servant leaders**.

It should be mentioned here that, in every place where Paul and his colleagues established house churches, they made it their duty to elect/select **Elders** to lead out in those churches. He even mentioned the qualifications needed to be applied in the selection of Elders in 1Timothy 3:1-7 and Titus 1:6-11 etc. In no place in his writing did Paul mention anyone in any other office who should supersede or be placed over the Elders in any church.

James, an Apostle of Christ referred to himself as an Elder and the servant/slave of Christ, and advised the twelve scattered tribes that if any among them was sick, *". . .He should call the elders of the church to pray over him and anoint him with oil in the name of the Lord"* (James 5:14, NIV). The apostles John and Peter settled down and eventually became Elders in their churches (2John 1:1; 3John 1:1 and 1Peter5:1). How difficult is this to comprehend that some of the disciples who walked with our Savior and were educated and trained by Him thought it not beneath them to be identified as Elders or Shepherd-servant leaders, not pastors, in the body of Christ.

The question that arises from this New Testament concept of those chosen for church leadership, Elders (Deacons also mentioned in Acts and 1Timothy 3:8-13), in the local churches who were ordained by God for that purpose is, why are they excluded from being the beneficiaries of the restructured distribution of the reinstated tithe and offerings if they are the biblically valid shepherd-servant church leaders in the New Dispensation? Remember, these are the ones who were selectively appointed to lead out in the Gentle churches after the death of Christ on the cross. So if the tithing law is still valid today, why is the tithe not utilized to reward these leaders for the work they do in the church? They are the ones (the Elders) who were divinely appointed by the Spirit of God working through Paul and others to select them for service in leadership roles as were the priests and Levites in the Old Testament temple.

For more in-depth information on biblical Elders (not Pastors and no derision is intended, only stating the biblical truth) being the Shepherd-servant leaders in the Christian Church, consult **The Unconventionality of Church Leadership: It Works**, pp. 165-171. It is so difficult to wrap one's mind around the change from Elder to Pastor leadership in the Christian era and one would definitely wonder, who was given that authority to make such a change? When one considers the fact that the book of Acts through 3John is replete with the idea of Elder leadership and the criteria for their selection in the New Testament Church versus one verse in Ephesians 4:11 that mentions "pastors," why the change? In addition, the Greek word for pastor means shepherd, and the only leaders, apart from the Disciples of Christ, who were instructed to shepherd God's flock are the Elders as was stated previously. So once again, I ask the questions, why are the biblically appointed indigenous leaders in each local Christian church excluded from sharing in the tithe if it is still extant? Who was given the authority to exclude them, and what was the underpinning rationale for the exclusion? Is divine authority given to each individual Christian denomination to make decisions that are contrary to the ordained biblical leadership structure? There are some denominations that have been honest and humble enough to acknowledge their mistake in the implementation of a pastoral system and have returned to the multiplicity of biblical Elder leadership.

Coming back to the information prior to my diversion, some may argue that the role of Israel was to become a godly nation at the intersection or crossroad of many nations so that they, the Gentile nations, would experience what God was really like and come to know Him as their God also. But as we are currently aware, Israel failed miserably. In addition, the functions of the priests and Levites were confined to the temple and not in preaching a gospel as is done in the Christian era. And it should be remembered that just as the Levites and priests were rewarded for their services in the Temple (God did not allow them to wait until they get to heaven to be rewarded as many are told today), the Elders and others spend long hours preparing to preach and perform other important roles in the church, so why are they not be rewarded with the resurrected tithes as are others?

There is no doubt that the mission of the Christian church is global in scope and requires much traveling and significant financial expenses. Christians do not function only as the body of Christ in a church building, but have a divine mandate to share the love of God with those who are not a part of His body. For those who are involved in the work of God on a global scale, the dissemination of the gospel to all nations, kindred, tongue and people, it is important to provide the necessary funding to finance their travel and modest accommodation. Any type of lavish spending to support a luxurious lifestyle in a work that calls for sacrifice, based on Jesus' example, has been and will be met with great skepticism and or withdrawal of funds.

One of the things that is so disturbing in many churches today is the use of a significant amount of funds to finance "choir" preaching in the name of body edification (so difficult to remember both topic and contents of sermons immediately after and in the long run) while the foot soldiers who labor by carrying the message of God's salvation and saving grace door to door and on foot, in rain and sunshine to the unsaved or un-churched, are left unrewarded for the most part.

Conclusion

The evidence presented in this chapter is a clear indication of the invalidity of the tithing principle transference from the O.T to the New Dispensation. The tithing passages in which Christ mentioned and supported the validity of the tithing precept is a clear indication that the tithing law/system was still "legally" binding then and to the point of His death on the cross.

That which cannot be overlooked is the apparent reduction in status of the said tithing principle as compared to the weightier matters of the law, such as mercy and justice etc.

Paul also mentioned the tithing concept in the book of Hebrews, but was he referring to its continuation or transference from the O.T. to the Christian era? As was mentioned earlier, he was addressing the Hebrew Christians who were being tempted to revert to Judaism. They had to be fully convinced that the old covenant with its sacrificial, priestly, and tithing laws no longer existed, in light of its continuation then in Judaism. It was within this historical context that Paul mentioned the tithe collected by the Levites etc. It was not presented as a new law or precept to be adhered to in the New Dispensation.

That which occurred in the sacrificial system was only a shadow of things pointing to the coming of the true Lamb of God. He, Jesus Christ, came and was offered up on the Cross as the supreme sacrificial Lamb, and subsequent to His resurrection, He is superior to Abraham, Moses and all the other prophets, angels and priests. He is their (our) High Priest and it was (is) to Him they looked for their redemption because there is no eternal future or spiritual value in turning back. In other words, His atoning death, resurrection and ascension created the path to the heavenly sanctuary where Christ is in the presence of God atoning for the sin of the entire world. There will never be another death and resurrection of Christ again, so why think about turning back?

It is decisively and unquestionably safe to conclude that the evidence presented in this chapter, based on the analysis of all New Testament passages referencing the tithing principle, does not support the transference and or applicability of that said principle in the New Dispensation or Christian era. There are a few passages mentioned by Jesus that have some relevance to the adherence of the tithing law, but that was before Christ died on the cross. The sacrificial system was still in operation and relevant during Jesus' life, but when He died on the cross and the Temple veil was rented from top to bottom, that brought to an end the old covenant and introduction of the new. This means that all facets of the sacrificial system, including the economic engine or tithing system, were abrogated at His death.

If this is not the case, why is there no evidence or scriptural proof that Christ, His disciple or any of the New Testament writers mentioned anything about the validity of the principle or was engaged in tithe paying prior to and or after the death of Christ? There is nothing written directly nor by implication about Jesus or His disciples paying tithe of anything that others contributed to their financial needs, and the law was in existence during His pre-crucifixion years.

In addition, I would assume that Paul, being a strict Pharisee, adhered to the tithing law prior to his dramatically enlightened experience with Jesus. If he did, then what caused him to abandon the idea or discontinue tithe paying. He was very conscious of his tribal roots as being from the Tribe of Benjamin. Not being related to the Levite tribe would disqualify him from any entitlement to the tithe. In addition, Paul knew that the Temple services with its High Priest and other priestly functionaries were made null and void by the death of Christ. And if their services were no longer needed or valid, so would the tithing law that was exclusively designed to support them. He, therefore, made no claim to, nor did he or any other N.T. writer recommend and or instruct the followers of Christ to adhere to the said principle in the New Dispensation.

If the tithing law was abolished or abrogated at the cross, and we know it was an element or component of the ceremonial laws, it has no relevance in God's church subsequent to Christ's crucifixion and extending into and beyond the twenty-first century. The New Testament church was and continues to be very different structurally from that of the O.T. church. Initially, it had financial needs and was in need of an economic system to support its services internally as well as externally. What are the new and relevant principles, means or methods of financing the operations of the body of Christ, His church, that are mentioned and or suggested/referenced in the New Testament for the New Dispensation? Let us examine the new N.T. paradigm of giving.

Chapter III

The New Paradigm of Giving

B ased on the lack of direct or indirect revelatory instructions and or teaching, and insufficient N.T. empirical or documentary evidence regarding the continuation of the tithing principle, or its transfer from the O.T. to the N.T. church, and the abrogation of the ceremonial laws at the death of Christ – inclusive of the priesthood, Levitical help, sacrificial sin offerings, and the tithing law, the latter of which served as its financial engine – and the global gospel commission directive given to the body of Christ that requires significant financing, what is the source of funding alluded to in the N.T. for the realization of such a monumental task?

In the book of Acts 2:44, 45 and 4:32-45, the new Christian believers commenced a revolutionary method of contributing to the work. Instead of adhering to the tithing law of ten percent, many believers sold their lands and houses, and gave all the money to the apostles who in turn distributed it according to the needs of the people. This initial action of the new converts (disciples) ushered in a new direction or emphasis on giving. It is unequivocally clear that the emphasis was on the creation of some semblance of equality of means by ascertaining the fulfillment of the needs of those who were economically impoverished.

These exceptionally generous members/disciples were Holy Spirit driven (filled with the Holy Ghost, Acts 4:31) and not law driven. If they had remained faithful to the antiquated tithing law, that approach would have been too restrictive and would have obligated them to give ten percent and an offering when they desired to give all. So they willingly, not as a result of some "legal" obligation, gave one hundred percent of their possessions and valuables. These were excellent stewards who realized that their possessions were not their own and that they had a sacred obligation to share in order to alleviate the suffering of their brothers and sisters who were less fortunate.

Unfortunately, this grand and exemplary action of the early Christians has been buried in the sands of time and replaced by a salary-driven service payment of those who decide and are selected or given the opportunity to enter full-time ministry. It can be assumed that the contributions of 100% of the early Christians were probably meant to be an ideally exemplary action to be duplicated by those Christians who can afford to do so in modern Christianity.

As was stated earlier, there is no direct or indirect instruction/ teaching in the New Testament regarding the transfer of or the survival of the economic support engine of the sacrificial system since Christ died on the cross. The entire system was abrogated, including the tithing law, and it can be safely concluded that Christians are not spiritually nor financially obligated to return a limited ten percent of their income to the church in the new covenantal dispensation of grace (John 1:17; Ephesians 2:5,8; Romans 3:24; 6:14).

Christians are Holy Spirit-driven people (Romans 8:14), especially those who seek Him, submit to and allow Him to reign supremely in their lives. They will allow themselves to be directed by Him on the basis of the giving principles outlined in the New Testament as to the amount or percentage of their income that should be contributed to the work of God. Those who still perceive the O.T. ten percent tithing law as the ceiling amount to be given (offerings are additional) are sadly mistaken and do not need the Spirit's guidance in this context if the law has already provided the amount to be contributed. If, however, that is still the law, why should Christians venture to exceed its limitation when the blessings will still come as a result of one's adherence to its inherent restriction(s). Or is it that one will receive more abundant blessings if one goes beyond that ceiling? If so, would that be the correct motive?

Some of the scriptural passages that provide Christians with a clear view or foundational principles of giving in the N.T. are those mentioned previously in Acts 2 and 4, and 11:27-30. In the latter text, a prophet named Agabus predicted a severe drought over all the Roman world and each of the disciples in Antioch provided relief/assistance to those living in Judea *"according to his ability"* (Acts 11:29, NIV). The above-mentioned texts and those to follow have no bearing or relevance to tithe paying and offerings as Christians know them today, but the principles underlying giving are clear indications as to how they should give in support of the work of God for the salvation of souls and *the sustenance of the poor which should not be an after thought subsequent to the end of a quarterly communion service.*

Paul is very clear in his instruction for Christians to give and to do so generously in order to meet the needs of God's people. He wrote, *"Share with God's people who are in need. Practice hospitality"* (Romans 12:13, NIV). This type of giving appears to have been a priority for Paul and was in harmony with what he did for the poor in the Jerusalem church. That which is striking in this passage is that Paul did not instruct the members to pay their tithes and offerings to the former Levites and priests functioning in their church. That system was completely annulled and inapplicable in the Christian era. Nor did he inform them to use the tithes and offerings to financially contribute to the assistance of their brethren. Instead, he encouraged them to willingly practice hospitality which is not based on a tithing law but on the goodness of their hearts as they are impressed by the Spirit of God.

The disciples gave according to their ability to contribute, and those of the Macedonian church gave even in their extreme poverty and *"...even beyond their ability"* (2Corinthians 8:3, NIV).

Paul mentioned several key points in reference to giving. There must be a willingness or willing mind to give based on that which one has and *"...not according to what he does not have"* in order to achieve the principle of equality (vs.13). The acceptability of the gift is based on the willingness to give it and what one can afford according to the Spirit's influence. God does not assess the value of the gift on the actual amount given but on the basis of the financial resources of the giver (Mark 12:41-44).

If Christians are limited, therefore, to a "legal" command of ten percent, how would God judge or measure the giving of people who are very wealthy and can give far in excess of the required 10% but are restricted by that law of giving? It should be stated unequivocally that the O.T. tithing law does not produce a willingness to give but a type of guilt avoidance and or a "loving compulsion" to give particularly when one is not in a position to contribute that amount but gives it anyway. God is certainly looking for willing givers in spite of the value placed on their gifts.

Paul wrapped up the content of the new paradigm of giving in 2 Corinthians 9:6, 7 (NIV):

> ***"Remember this: whosoever sows sparingly will also reap sparingly, and whoever sows generously will also reap generously.***
>
> ***Each man should give what he has decided in his heart to give, not reluctantly or under compulsion, for God loves a cheerful giver."***

Inclusive in this passage of scripture is a significant principle of what the author refers to as a natural law of life and that is, ***"what a person sows is what he/she will reap"*** (Galatians 6:7). A farmer does not sow wheat and expects to reap oranges. Nor will he/she sow cotton and expect to reap apples. A person who lives an unholy life does not expect to inherit eternal life in the hereafter unless there is some mental instability or derangement. The person who lives a stingy life in reference to how others are treated by him/her financially and otherwise, should not expect the generosity of others or the blessings of God (Proverbs 22:9). People are generally inclined to treat others as they are being treated. On the other hand, people who are known to have little or no means, or fall in the poverty category on the economic scale but are generous in what they can afford, are generally reacted to with great generosity when others are called upon to assist them.

In addition, our heavenly Father knows our financial conditions and understands our motives in giving. He knows when we are generous with His/our possessions in reference to our response in meeting the financial needs of others and His cause. And it is difficult to understand how He will reward someone generously when that person was just the opposite. God was and continues to be very generous towards the human family in giving His Son to die for its/our redemption, and He expects us to be willingly generous to each other, for in so doing, we are being generous to Him. Nothing should be too valuable that it cannot be given to Him and His cause based on our love for Him and our willingness to contribute to His work.

Paul has also included in his paradigm of giving the concept of the **individual's freedom to choose/decide** in his/her heart (influenced by the Spirit of God) that which he/she should give. And this decision should be made voluntarily and not through any externally compulsive dictate (See Acts 11:29; 1Cor. 16:2). In other words, giving should not be based on any external force or legal imposition but should result from an inward resolve influenced by the Holy Spirit to give, and once that is done, the giving or presenting of our gifts will be a cheerful experience and this is the attitude that God appreciates and rewards.

On the other hand, the tithing law which some claim to have survived the cross would be a classic contradiction to what Paul is proposing in reference to giving. It is an external force impacting upon the decision of the individual giver thus resulting in giving based on a law (although some can give out of love for the law), a situation that would extract the cheerfulness from the giving particularly if one is not in a position to give the required "legal" amount. Such giving would benefit the beneficiaries of the church organization but for the giver, it would be an act in futility since the gift would not be acceptable to God because He loves a cheerful giver.

Also, those who return/give the tithe and offering based on the expectation of a blessing in return from God may be obeying an obsolete law compounded with the wrong motive, and this would also be unacceptable to Him. This is an idea that is over emphasized in some churches. *"Give and it will be given unto you"* appears to be a foundational principle of giving that is generally attached to the promotion of tithe giving as an incentive to give generously. Does the implication in this incentive to give involve an ulterior motive for giving? Why should Christians not give out of their love for God and the goodness of their hearts, in order to contribute to a sufficiently financial provision for the realization of the gospel commission into all the world. God blesses us every day with life, health, strength, abilities to see, hear, walk and talk, to earn a living at which economic level it may be, so why should we expect anything else in return for that which we give? The expectation of giving in anticipation of receiving something in return appears to be tantamount to the application of the wrong motive to a magnificently noble cause.

The principles of giving proposed by Paul make such great sense especially when applied to those who fall in the lower and lowest end of the socio-economic scale. There are so many poor people (and the majority of those who accept Christ as their Lord are relatively poor) who are faced with government taxes, high rent, high cost of heating and air conditioning, food, transportation etc., the cost of which their salaries or wages are insufficient to cover. But they are expected to return a tithe and give an offering while the church ignores their financial plight due to the insensitivity of the members and leaders, and the absence of a structured budgetary provision to meet such needs.

Members should not be blamed for the latter situation. It appears to be the result of the long established system that has directed their mind in the direction of ignoring the poor amongst them. The emphases were and continue to be placed on collecting the tithe to pay the salaries of the so-called "full-time gospel preachers etc." and the offerings for the programmatic operations of the local churches while the poor were and still go unnoticed.

That which is still so heart wrenching was to see a poor family sacrifice the little they had to support those who were financially better off. That particular family of six or seven really struggled financially due to an extreme situation that befell one of the parents. They embarrassingly moved from one small home to another in their attempt to escape the serious deterioration of the previous ones that the landlords refused to repair. In spite of their economic situation, the mother continued to return a faithful tithe and offering to the church to reward those who did not put in the time of the workers in the Temple. And that which was so disheartening was to see some men of the cloth have their clothes washed by that mother with no reward for her labor. That family's plight was so blatantly obvious and the church never stepped in to provide any assistance. If there is any blame to be laid at anyone's feet, it is that of the leaders and established system. Things or subject matters that should have been emphasized relatively regularly in sermons and other presentations were completely neglected and or ignored, and the family truly suffered. This needs to change!!

In addition, the poor attend church services and are made to feel so guilty because of their inability to return ten percent of their earnings. So they worship God with a guilty conscience and probably leave the services feeling spiritually empty and some may, after feeling that way for a time, just do not return especially after hearing the story of the Widow who threw in all that she had in the Temple treasury. And what is so intriguing about this story is Christ's comment that she had given more than those who gave far in excess of her sacrificial contribution, a farthing. Should this unique situation be used by Christian leaders to encourage poor Christians, many of whom may be as poor as the Widow by today's economic standards, to give until it hurts even all they have and be left in the economic cold? You decide!

The reasons behind the Widow's mite is understandable in its uniquely historical and social/spiritual context, but based on other scriptural passages, it is not the general expectation of Christ for His people to pour all their earnings into the church and leave themselves economically vulnerable. He expects us to use our God-given transcendental common sense and create some equilibrium or balance in the totality of our lives, including the economic aspect of it.

As people of faith, rich or poor, we acknowledge God's ownership of everything given to us and that we should be excellent stewards of His property. He, however, does not need "our" money but our souls. This is not to suggest that the poor or very poverty-stricken people are restricted or exempt from making financial contributions to the cause of God or the church if they are in a position to do so. They have a spiritual obligation to contribute on the basis of the giving principles outlined by Paul in the new paradigm of giving. They should be allowed to determine in their hearts/minds through the influence of the Spirit of God that which they can give based on what they possess and not on that which they do not have. Tithing, if still extant, would impose upon them an external law to give that which they probably could not afford and would create further economic hardship on such people. This would make them guilty in the presence of God during the collective worship in the body of Christ, His church. This would be an unsatisfactory and unfulfilling time of worship, and an exceptionally sad situation to ponder.

Why Should Christians Give?

As was mentioned earlier, the commission pronounced by Christ to His disciples is radically different to the mission of Israel in the Old Testament, and that said commission is relevant to His disciples today. We are told to "go", not wait for the world to come to us, and make disciples for Jesus by teaching all nations about His reconciling work and second coming, and the need for all people to align their lives with his kingdom principles through the power of the Holy Spirit of God.

Unfortunately, the mission has been diluted to mean, to go and make church members. Members go to church a day or two per week without any involvement in the mission to go and teach all nations including the one of which we are a part. If the emphasis was on making disciples, quality would have taken precedence over quantity and the "numbers game" would have no relevance in our evangelistic efforts and it should not, because it is the Spirit of God who influences souls or people to come to Jesus. We may sow the seeds and water the ground, but it is the Spirit of God who makes things grow and does the reaping or gives the increase (1 Corinthians 3:6-9).

The reality for many in the short run is that numbers look good on paper and boost their standing/ratings in the eyes of the administrators who forget that God does the reaping. The flip side to the "numbers game" is that too many people are pressured in a short period of time, without a comprehensive understanding of what it means to be a genuine disciple, to go into the pool or be baptized only to emerge with no further disciple support, training or educational program for the further development of those disciples. The result is more than tragic since too many walk out the back door of the church yearly never to return.

When we, therefore, consider the thousands of dollars spent annually on evangelistic crusades, do we get a good enough "bang for the buck"? Some people may rationalize that any amount of money spent to save one soul is well spent dollars. A reasonable response is that many people are led to Christ yearly without the expenditure of a single dollar. This is done on the basis of a one-and-one contact. Members getting involved in an economically deprived or moneyless outreach program for Jesus based on their relationship with Him and the empowerment of the Holy Spirit, and building healthy functional relationships with family members and friends. This is more likely to produce greater and more lasting results than those one-, two- and or six-week evangelistic crusades.

The absence of the "numbers game" means that the number of converts may be smaller on paper and not good enough to boost the evangelist's ego and or ratings from an administrative perspective, but in the long run, disciples stay in the church, walk in the Master's footsteps through the alignment of their lives with His teachings and are fully engaged in the making of other disciples. Initially, the number may appear smaller, but the multiplication of disciples may be exponential due to the consistent involvement of a greater percentage of members or disciples in gospel dissemination and a much reduced attrition rate. This can become a new reality since disciples are less dependent on clergy and more dependent on the Holy Spirit of God.

The current reality in North America does not alter the commission to go, but it needs to be transformed in order to change the misconceived philosophy of some people in the church that it is an end in itself which may be a function of the institutionalization of the gospel and the professionalization of the ministry. It can be safely assumed, based on Christian theology, that Jesus' view of the church is that it is a means to an end, organized for the effectuation of a very special kingdom-building mission, and not an end in itself.

As a combination of these, it appears that the church has effectively lost that early-church spirit of voluntarism in which no one was paid for his/her functional contributions in carrying the work forward internally and externally except for a few supported evangelists. In the modern church, however, there is one professional group of individuals or Christians, including administrators and their staff members, who is paid for its services while practically all others volunteer their time. This special arrangement seems to contradict that which God instituted in Israel with the Levites and Aaronic priests. They all were rewarded with the tithes and offerings as a payment for their services, so why the dramatic change if the tithing law is still extant.

In addition, many seem to think that it is the sole responsibility of the one paid (clergy/pastors) for his/her services to take the gospel to the community due to the amount of time he/she has available weekly, and such a rationale is understandable. If, however, a disciple-based church is given greater credence or serious consideration over a member-based church, this may change such a perception for the greater involvement of all in the gospel dissemination, and particularly if those responsible for the care of the church, the Elders etc., are paid for their services.

The reality of the world in which we live demands that numerous Christian disciples work two and three jobs just to maintain a roof over their heads and supply food for their family tables. This means that too many Christians are overwhelmingly too busy or distracted with the mundane things to be meaningfully involved in sharing the gospel on a large-scale basis. They need to seek those opportunities at work, on the train or bus and in between work to share the love of God with others.

A greater share of the burden in gospel proclamation is assigned to those who have chosen and given the opportunity to be engaged honestly in gospel dissemination in foreign and their native lands. They deserve economic care. Those who are dishonest or do not take their sacred responsibility seriously, or those who are just preaching to the "choir" weekly with no serious involvement with the unsaved or un-churched need to be recognized as part-time workers. In other words, Christians should give generously to support the work of Christ or all those who are honestly engaged in the continuation of His ministry of reconciliation, or the gospel ministry on a full-time basis.

In addition to this significant ministry support, the church local and administrators at the administrative levels need to structure a sizable portion of its budget for the support of the needy in their con-gregations, and find a confidential method of discovering those who are in need and help them. It should be borne in mind that too many of those who need help are reluctant to ask. Many of these have lived relatively independent lives for years and are too ashamed to admit they need assistance, but they do. It was a priority of the early church and its example stands as an exemplary monument to be imitated in our post-modern age. It is a sacred responsibility and one that needs to be reinstated in the modern church. It is an aspect of our practical Christianity for which God will eventually hold us accountable.

There are other causes and or projects (including church building maintenance etc.) to which Christians should give, but from a biblical perspective, the two mentioned above are the most significant to which disciples should contribute their finances. And they should do so because of their role recognition as good stewards of God's property. In other words, they are cognizant that *"The earth is the Lord's, and everything in it, the world, and all who live in it"* (Psalms 24:1, NIV), and that they are charged with the responsibility of administering His possessions in a way that will bring glory to His name. ***"Each one should use whatever gift he has received to serve others, faithfully administering God's grace in its various forms"*** (1Peter 4:10, NIV).

Christians are also to give based on the impelling model of **generosity** introduced by Christ in the sacrificial gift of His life, the ultimate sacrifice, for the redemption of the human family. ***"For you know the grace of our Lord Jesus, that though he was rich, yet for your sakes he became poor, so that you through his poverty might become rich"*** **(2Corinthians 8:9, NIV).** This is not to suggest that because our Savior gave or sacrificed His all, His life, for us that we should give everything to His cause and neglect our families. It is very important for Christians to attempt to create an equilibrium or balance in the administration of their finances. Christ would never want anyone to collect a pay check, donate it all to His work and deprive his/her family members of the necessities of life such as a roof, food and clothing. He wants us to exercise our transcendental uncommon sense and take care of our family members who are a very significant part of His cause and ministry.

Christ does not want to impose a limit, upper or lower, upon our giving in the New Dispensation that will place a damper on the influence of the Holy Spirit in reference to how much influence He will exert on us to give due to His perfect knowledge of what He knows we can give. Some members or people may be able to give their full paychecks based on their financial situation, and may be in a good position to give with great ease the ten percent as some believe is required without the Spirit's influence. Christ wants us to listen to the voice of the Holy Ghost and decide in our minds the amount to be given as God prospers us. Whatever is given and it may be all of one's possession (100%), or it may exceed the ten percent many times, but it must be based on the individual's decision for each will have to give an account to Him for his/her stewardship (Romans 14:12).

In addition, once the individual decision is made without any legally external imposition or compulsion, the giver is to present his/ her gift to God or His cause with a **willing mind**. If the willingness is absent, according to Paul in 2Corinthians 8:12, the gift will not be acceptable to God and He is the only One to whom we are accountable. When people give unwillingly or reluctantly the externally imposed tithe as some think is still obligatory, man does not generally see the reluctantly grudging facial expression or motive of the giver, or deep emotional pain associated with placing the unaffordable gift in the offering plate that makes the person feel at ease in the sight of man for his or her compliance with the expectation of paying tithe. Unfortunately, the gift is unacceptable in the sight of God for their inability to afford that amount as well as the unwillingness in giving the gift as was stated earlier.

Christians are responsible for pleasing God first in spite of and irrespective of how other Christians feel about their attitude towards or behavior in giving. Man will look on the externals and the church books, and determine that you are not contributing sufficiently to the cause, but the giver must be convinced and or persuaded in his/her heart/mind that God is pleased with the gifts presented.

Giving in the dispensation of grace is influenced by the Holy Spirit and based on the principles of **cheerful willingness** (willing mind) and **generosity** within the context of **proportionality**. It is not done in the extreme for self-aggrandizement in order to attract compliments about our gifts; nor is it done for self or family deprivation; nor for the enrichment of some and impoverishment of others in the church since such a situation will prolong the economic inequality among God's people and help to nullify an important reason for which He died. Christians are to give in order to meet the needs of the less fortunate and for those who have chosen to genuinely engage in full-time or part-time gospel ministry. As are guided by the Holy Spirit, we are to give based on what we have and not on that which we do not have.

It, giving, is to be done willingly and not because of any undue external pressure. In so doing, we are giving a part of ourselves to God which may be indicative of a truly magnanimous character and the noblest kind of giving as was demonstrated by Christ on the cross for the human family. In conjunction with financial offerings, we are to give ourselves as living sacrifices to Him which is the ultimate gift to God. We need to be mindful that some may be giving large gifts to God or His cause while giving their souls to someone else. This is a situation that all Christians need to avoid at all cost.

The Irrelevance of Priests and Tithing in the New Order of the Christian Church

The new order of the Christian church is radically different from that of the Old Testament church. It has no need for earthly Sanctuary-functioning priests and high priests, mediators between God and generic man because the sacrificial system of the old order was abrogated at the cross with the sacrifice of the perfect Lamb of God, Jesus Christ. This act made Him our High Priest and us His disciples or converts as priests according to the book of Peter.

The abrogation of the ceremonial laws simultaneously annulled the sanctuary structure and services, and the purpose for which it was designed; the priesthood; Levitical helpers; sacrificial sin offerings and the tithing law as was mentioned previously. Unfortunately, many denominational bodies and individuals continue to think of the tithing law as an independent principle that was instituted prior to its inclusion in the O.T. sacrificial system; that it was applied to such a system as its economic support temporally, and when that system was abolished, the tithing principle survived and continues to be a significant law to be applied in the New Dispensation or Christian era.

I heard a preacher on television communicating this same concept of the tithe being an independent law or principle that was not annulled but survived the cross. But what did he mean by it being independent? A classical definition of "independent" would mean a person, thing or concept who or that is free from the influence, control, support, authority or jurisdiction of another. Based on this definition, it appears that the tithing law was created in a vacuum, and laws are not developed for the sake of laws articulation. There are natural laws that were put in place by the Creator when He created the universe. They were not created in a vacuum, but for the purpose of chaos avoidance while providing some control or operational guidance in how the universe functions. Human laws are also not created in a vacuum but within a socio-economic contextual reality that provide guidelines or norms that are intended to govern and or produce specifically desired behavioral outcomes in human interactions.

The tithing law was not created in a vacuum as an independent entity, but for some specific purpose(s) in a socio-religious context that is probably unknown to us due to the lack of historical and or biblical documentation. That which is so fascinating is God's application of the tithing law to the sacrificial system in the O.T. This provides us with an applicable context of the law and suggests or indicates a prior precedential circumstance(s) for such a law.

Let me repeat again for emphasis that there was a pre-Israel tithing practice and that it, the tithe, was apparently used to support a priest(s) since Abram gave a tithe to Melchizedek, the king and priest of Salem. But was this priest/king in charge of an organized religious system of worship? Did he, Melchizedek, have assistants and was the tithe shared with the said priestly helpers? If there were no helpers and the priests were the only ones entitled to the tithe, why does it appear that God contravened His law and included or gave it, the tithe (90% of it) to the Levites who were not priests and only ten percent to the priests when the law was applied to or included as a component in the institutionalization of the sacrificial system?

As was mentioned previously, God is the Owner of everything and He has the authority to apply what is His to anyone or cause as He sees appropriate. So whether the tithing law was in existence prior to Israel becoming a free or theocratic nation has no real relevance in terms of providing it with immunity from abrogation. The priestly and animal sacrifice laws appear to be independent entities also because they existed prior to Israel becoming a nation of God's people with a sacrificial system of worship, yet they were annulled by the death of their Creator on the cross. What seems to be of greater significance is the annulment of a system and the creation of a totally new one with the application of the old economic support system surviving and being applied or transplanted to the new without any biblical or New Testament evidentiary reference to its survival and application.

This idea can be compared to the putting of new wine in old bottles. It is very difficult to understand the logics of the survival of the tithing law in the absence of a theological and or N.T. teaching or explanation, and in light of the dissolution of both the priestly and animal sacrifice laws. If there was no sanctuary, there would have been no institutionalized sacrificial system. And the abolition of the sacrificial sin offerings means that there is no need for O.T. priestly and Levitical functionaries; and if there is no need for priests and Levites, it logically follows that there is no need for a tithing law due to its purpose expiration and or a complete dissolution of the system in which it was applied. They, all the components of the sacrificial system, were all interrelated, intertwined and therefore inseparable upon their institutionalization in the economy of Israel. The system would have become very dysfunctional if only one component was absent or extracted from it. When the system was made obsolete, no one component survived for the purpose of its transference to another as was previously stated.

Some people may be inclined to believe that this line of reasoning is the fatal flaw in the argument and or proposition of this book due to the existence of a tithing practice intimated by the actions of Abram and Jacob as mentioned earlier in this book. Exclusive of these two occurrences, the tithing law was introduced in Israel through its exclusive linkage to the Levites and priests, and it remained in that state all through the O.T. to the death of Christ on the cross. The tithing law was never linked or connected to any other person or group of people in both the Old and New Testaments.

With the annulment of one came the abrogation of all. If this is illogical or theologically incorrect, where is the biblical proof to invalidate this line of reasoning? If this is not the case, why didn't Jesus, Paul nor any other N.T. writer provide any instruction in this regard, or wrote about any other being engaged in compliance through their actions with the tithing law?

The opportunities for them to have done so were numerous as they wrote about the collection of offerings for the poor etc., and even when Paul mentioned the comparison of the priests being fed from the altar, yet he failed to provide a link to the application of the tithing law in the new Christian era. Is it that Paul was acutely aware of the original purpose of the tithe and was unsure as to its application in the New Dispensation era? Or was it a certainty that the death of Christ obliterated it at the cross and there has been no biblical change in, nor substitution of that law.

There is no doubt that there was direct instruction in regards to the tithing law application in the Old Testament. The tithes belonged to God and He assigned it to the Levites with a small portion going to the priests. This was so arranged in order to reward them for their services in the Temple. And to reiterate, the Levites could not be priests regardless of any inner compulsion or feeling of a calling to the priesthood. There was a clear dividing line drawn in the sand. An appropriately modern expression is to say that **there was an unbreakable glass ceiling** beyond which no other, except those appointed, could pass. It was quite a rigid system and could not survive the rigorous scrutiny of the New Dispensation that embraced both Jews and Gentiles. This glass ceiling would have kept Gentiles in an inferior position in God's church and it had to be abandoned in order to accommodate a new quality state of being and thought.

In the Christian church, there is no Jew nor Gentile, male nor female. There is no division of members based on office, family, tribe, function, economics, education etc.; all are equal in the sight of God. As was said previously, the Spirit of God has endowed all members with a diversity of gifts and no gift is of greater significance than the other. All are expected to work cooperatively for the realization of the will of God in His church. So what are the functional differences between the spiritual leaders in the Old Testament Church versus those of the Christian Church that warranted or justified the annulment of the offerings and tithing law at the cross?

There were always a High Priest and other priests who were selected to serve the spiritual needs of the Israelites. The primary function of the High Priest was to appear before God in the Most Holy Place of the Temple as the reconciling mediator between Him and His people. Once per year, he presented a sin offering for himself and one for the people on the Day of Atonement. The priests also functioned primarily in a mediatorial role on behalf of the Israelites on a daily basis through their acceptance and participation in the offering of each individual's animal sin sacrifice etc. And there were about three services that were conducted within the restricted space of the Temple and court yard by the priests and their helpers. This means that these chosen men had to be present at the Temple to conduct the services on a daily basis. This is probably the, or one of the reasons why they were paid with the tithe and offerings, a relatively secured source of funding, for their services. This required their full-time attention and time, and they were not allowed to pursue any other line of work.

Let us fast forward to the spiritual leaders, according to the Word of God, the Apostles, Deacons and Elders or shepherd-servant leaders of the New Testament church. Their primary functions were:

1. The proclamation of the gospel message to the Jews and Gentiles, as was clearly demonstrated in the work of the disciples, Paul and others, and
2. Taking care of the poor, as was done by the Jerusalem Church (food distribution) and Paul in his collection of offerings for the poor in the Jerusalem Church.

Over the years, between the early Christian church and the twenty-first century, there have been some additions to those primary functions. These are as follows:

1. **building up or edification of the body of Christ in preparation for internal and external service,**
2. **advancing the gospel commission** into all the world through the human empowerment by the Holy Spirit,
3. **rites of baptism,** and
4. **the Lord's Supper.**

These major functions are not conducted primarily by the leaders of the Christian church. There are always other members who participate in and at times, lead out in the performance of these roles. These New Testament leaders, Elders according to the N.T. and pastors according to many religious organizations are of no greater value to the functions performed by the other members. Yet, it is the modern-day appointed pastors who are classified as a type of priest. But what real purpose does it serve for such a classification when all of God's people are priests according to 1Peter 2:9?

Fortunately, no human being, pastor, Elder or any one else, can function as a mediator between man and God. And certainly, there is no human or professional category of humans who can be classified as a High Priest(s). Christ is our only High Priest and He paid the ultimate price or cost of our redemption with His life when He bore the sin of humanity to the cross. He earned that office and it cannot be transferred and or occupied by any human being.

All of God's people have direct access to the Father through Jesus Christ our heavenly High Priest and Mediator. They (we) are assigned the "office" of a holy priesthood "*. . .to offer up spiritual sacrifices, acceptable to God by Jesus Christ*" (1Pet. 2:5), and those sacrifices appear to be that which His people are commissioned to "*. . . present your {their} bodies a living sacrifice, holy, acceptable unto God, which is our reasonable service*" (Rom.1: 12, JJKV). If this is the case of reality for all Christians, then why the typological study(ies) resulting in the subjective conclusion of the pastors being a type of priest. It is futile.

As can be readily deduced from the above information, the functional nature and time requirements of the spiritual leaders of both systems are significantly different. The functions of the N.T. leaders are not conducted on a daily basis within the confines of a physical structure as were those of the Temple. Christian spiritual leaders have a tremendous amount of flexibility and can select the times and days when they choose to operate, except when functioning in or performing certain established time-sensitive services in church buildings.

Therefore, whether one (or many) is preaching or teaching, there is no biblically imposed restrictions on when and how these roles are to be conducted. There is also no such biblically restrictive imposition for the full-time employment of those who choose to participate in the dissemination of the gospel. Based on the above and previous information, it appears that there is no need for full-time personnel as was needed in the Temple. The Christian Church or body of Christ seems to need a different economic system due to its all-member priesthood and the responsibility of all to be involved in the work of global gospel proclamation. What do you think? Do you believe these are the only justifications for the non-transference of the tithing law in the N.T. church? Or do you believe that the appointment of "full-time pastors" warranted the transference and application of the tithing principle in some present-day Christian denominations?

Before you arrive at a definitive conclusion, let us continue the discussion. There is both an internal and external mission. The major external focal mission of the Christian church is gospel proclamation to all nations for the creation of disciples or followers of Christ and the saving of their souls in God's kingdom. Some think that the realization of such a mission requires full-time preachers, but the author is convinced that it takes all of God's children or disciples working in concert with the Holy Spirit to accomplish such a monumental goal. However, based on the current system or church organization, those who have chosen and have been selected to perform a full-time role in the realization of this goal, need to be financially supported through voluntary, cheerful and generous contributions based on the principles of giving outlined by Paul since there is no direct tithing teaching given or presented for their sustenance.

If, however, all converted disciples were actively engaged in fulfilling their roles in this mission actualization, why would there be a need for such support? Is Paul's work ethics an exemplary model to be applied in the year 2017? He affirmed unequivocally through his own example that there is no biblically restrictive imposition of full-time employment in another field placed on anyone who chooses to be a gospel proclaimer. He truly sacrificed by working a tent–making job to support himself and colleagues while volunteering his services in full-time gospel preaching or evangelism. And in spite of his circumstances, no other earthly human being has made as significant a contribution to gospel dissemination as he did by the grace of God. Is it not that which is done by members who go house to house as well as meeting people on a one-on–one basis on the streets while they work full-time jobs to support their families? Why should this be the expectation for "ordinary" church members while the expectation is lower for those paid for their "full-time services" in ministry?

Many leaders claim that their role is to teach members how to witness for Jesus, but they conveniently forget to remember how Jesus taught His disciples. He was more than involved in the process. He did not verbalize alone or taught in theological abstraction and then sent out His disciples to practice on the streets, but clearly demonstrated the needed skills and dependence on the Spirit of God to accomplish the mission. In other words, Jesus was there with His disciples on the street, meeting the people, mingling with them, feeling their pain, relieving their hunger etc. He taught them in the School of Hard Knocks, on the job training, not from a pulpit or in a secluded classroom only. When He was through, He sent them two by two.

It should be noted here also, that no one can claim to have been selected by God to serve in any special or superior capacity as were the Levites and priests. And, therefore, no one has the God-given rights to the tithes or offerings if they are still extant because no one can claim to be a descendent of the Levite tribe or Aaron and his father's family. The original tithe was specifically set aside by God as a reward for the full-time services of these men and their families, and no one has that genealogical link to that tribe since the vast majority of Christians are Gentiles.

It is very difficult to comprehend that no other Jew from any of the eleven tribes in Israel could or had the God-given authority to collect tithes from their fellow Jews, except for the Levites. If this was the reality and it was, then how can Christians, Gentiles or non-Jewish followers of Christ even begin to think that they have the authority from God to collect tithes from both Jews and Gentiles? Unfortunately, the law that provided the exclusive right for the Levites to collect tithes has not changed nor was it transferred to the Christian era. It was nailed to and nullified at the cross with all the other sacrificial laws as was stated earlier. This means that no Christian, Gentile nor Jewish descendant, has a right or is allowed to collect any tithe from anyone in the New Dispensation.

In addition, Christian disciples are Holy-Spirit driven and are expected to be involved in sharing the love of God with unbelievers/ un-churched. We are endowed by the Spirit with diverse gifts for the building up of the saints in preparation for service and maturity in Christ. Why should some of the saints such as pastors, musicians, secretaries, custodians and others be paid for their services while others are expected to volunteer their time? Unless there is consistency in reference to an all-member volunteer evangelistic force for Christ, there will always be murmuring against those who are paid for their services.

One of the important problems with this pay for selective services is that it has been abused by so many. There are those who have the gift of preaching and desire to be paid when they preach in an evangelistic crusade or on TV, and many demand considerable sums of money as payment in addition to their salaries. I heard of a preacher who was paid $6,000.00 to preach in a three-week evangelistic crusade which amounts over $300.00 per sermon, since his lodging and meals are normally excluded from the preaching fee. Is he in the preaching business to make money as a peddler of the gospel?

Difficult to say or judge since the power to read his motive is absent, but there are those in gospel ministry just for the perceived prestige and money. And there are numerous preachers who have accumulated

185

a tremendous amount of wealth. Some have become so rich that they can afford to live in multi-million dollar homes, fly in their personal jets, and drive in some of the most expensive cars (check the internet for the accumulated wealth of those popular preachers and you will be amazed). Yet they continue to call for the tithe and offerings to finance their lavish life-style.

It does appear that such an approach and expenditure of funds are nothing more than an abuse of money received in the name of God while the poor continue to suffer and are neglected. This is a very sad picture and needs to be radically transformed to reflect the model of giving in the early New Testament church, and the purpose for which it was contributed.

Paid Clergy – Tithing Reinstatement

It appears that there is an exceptionally strong correlation between paid clergy and the reinstatement of the Old Testament tithing law or principle in many Christian churches. In other words, those churches that have selected to pay their pastors/ministers for their "full-time services" are generally the ones that have reinstated the said tithing law due to its consistency and dependability in terms of the flow of funds on a regular basis. On the other hand, those churches that have no paid clergy are generally the ones that do not see the theological relevance and or the link between the Old Testament tithing law and giving in the New Dispensation.

There are also those who believe that a system of paid clergy is far more effective in gospel proclamation or reaching the unsaved than having an all-volunteer force. A snapshot or superficial examination of the first Church in Rome that morphed into the Roman Catholic Church and became the predominant Christian Church reveals that it has no paid clergy. Yet, it has a global reach and has "converted" millions to Catholicism over hundreds of years which is a significant accomplishment regardless of the methods employed which are not in question here.

That which is also very surprising is the vast number of brilliant theologians in that church who did not conclude over the years that there is some theological mandate to transfer the tithing law from the O.T to the N.T. and implement it in their church. This is not to suggest that some have not tried over the years to apply the principle in their effort to raise money for the operation of that church. It just did not win over or convinced the majority of important decision makers in Catholicism for this concept to have taken deep roots and remain a significant and justifiable "legal" means of raising church funds.

In addition to the above, there are other Christian denominations such as The World Wide Church of God, the Jehovah Witness and the Mormons that have no paid clergy (based on my current knowledge) and are some of the fastest growing churches on a world-wide basis. Base on the author's limited knowledge of the latter two, they seem to have such a motivated and committed volunteer-member force that hit the pavement going house to house, making contact and influencing people through their personal interaction with those contacted. This method appears to be very effective and is in alignment with the N.T. evangelistic model (Jesus' model), and one that deserves further study and implementation.

Does this approach in reference to the all-volunteer or all-member force and the non-application of the tithing law among these churches mean that they have arrived at the correct theological conclusion that the tithing law was a component of the sacrificial laws and abrogated at the cross? The absence of any theological instruction in reference to the transference and application of the tithing law, subsequent to the death of Christ on the cross in the N.T., seems to validate their conclusion and practice today.

Based on scriptural evidence, the tithing law was first given to Israel through its leaders who kept meticulous records of the descendents' genealogical connection to the Levite tribe and particularly to that of the Aaronic priests due to the fact that tithes were paid only to these two groups of people. However, when Jerusalem, as was predicted by Jesus, was destroyed by the Roman Empire in A.D. 70, it brought about the total destruction of the Temple and all the priestly genealogical records. As a result, the tithing system came to an end because no one in Judaism could accept tithes except those appointed by God, the Levites.

As a result of the Temple's obliteration, it appears that there would have been no more collection of tithes, even in modern Jewish synagogues and or "temples." I discovered from a Jewish man with whom I spoke, that there is no one single acceptable method of financing their operations. There are some synagogues that accept tithes while others do not. Those that do not, as well as those who do, depend also on the free-will donations of their members as well as funds collected from members who pay to occupy certain seats during synagogue worship and on other occasions. There is no theological mandate to pay a tithe and give offerings. Funds collected for the operations of the synagogues are voluntarily donated.

If they are still collecting tithes, even though on a voluntary basis, is that an indication that they are following the O.T. tithing law and to what extent? Did they discover the lost genealogical records from the destroyed Temple in Jerusalem? Or was someone or some people given a revelation with the knowledge and or information of all those who are connected genealogically to the Levites? Or is it that they are not strictly adhering to the tithing law as was given by God to Israel but have employed greater flexibility in their interpretation of the said principle? Or is it because they are not required but that it is given on a voluntary basis? Or maybe they are cognizant of its annulment when Christ died on the cross? Or are they as some Christians who just believe in the continuation of the tithing law? If it is, however, that they do not believe in the coming and crucifixion of Jesus as the Messiah, then I can understand their unknown rationale for the continued adherence to the antiquated law.

As was mentioned earlier, some people in certain denominations believe in the necessity of the tithing principle as a very dependable source of income for the payment of their clergy and others in order to advance the gospel proclamation to all the world. Based, however, on the rapid growth of certain none-paid clergy denominations, one begins to question the real significance of paid clergy in this context. Particularly when one realizes that the focus of modern-day preaching is quite different to that of the early church.

In Acts 6:1-7, when the seven deacons were chosen to oversee the "daily distribution of food" due to the complaints of the Grecian

Jews, the Apostles did not want to be distracted from their preaching to the unsaved, so the daily internal administration of the church was turned over to the deacons. This focused preaching on the unsaved was not designed for the current converts but for those outside the body of Christ. It was all-year round evangelism, unlike that of what Christians experience today. Many currently concentrate on evangelistic preaching for a short period of time annually, but for the Apostles, it was a daily activity, preaching to those who needed to hear about God's saving grace in a very law-oriented society, not those who already knew about Jesus.

It is so difficult to escape the fact that in the late twentieth and early twenty-first centuries, billions of dollars have been spent to pay clerics to preach to the "choir" or those who already know the gospel while the unsaved, to a large extent, continue to languish due to the relative negligence to undertake the greater responsibility to go and make disciples of the unsaved for Jesus. There needs to be, just as Jesus and the Apostles did, a more significant emphasis placed on reaching to the unsaved than that which is focused on those who are already in the process of being saved.

Conclusion

People of the Christian faith will generally recognize the theological or scriptural evidence that God, through Moses and Aaron, instituted the O.T. sacrificial system which included the sanctuary, priesthood, Levitical helpers, sacrificial sin offerings, tithing and all the other ceremonial laws for the spiritually effective operation of the system.

This seems to suggest that if there was no instituted sacrificial system, there would have been no implementation of a tithing law in Israel. In other words, there would have been no rationale to establish a tithing principle without a sacrificial system and the reverse. To say the least, the tithing law was the underpinning economic or financial principle or engine that sustained the said system of worship and it was designed, and or implemented for that specific purpose only. All the components of the system were interrelated and interdependent which means that if one was annulled, the entire system would have disintegrated or fallen apart.

It was also God's intent for the Levites to be *"... responsible for the care of the Tent of Meeting – all the work at the Tent – and no one else may come near where you are"* (Numbers 18:4, NIV), and also to *"... bear the responsibility for offenses against it"* (ve.23) while Aaron, his sons and his father's household were to serve *"...as priest in connection with everything at the altar and inside the curtain. I am giving you the service of the priesthood as a gift"* (vs. 7 or 18:17). *"Anyone else who comes near the sanctuary must be put to death"* (vs. 7). In other words, Aaron, his sons and descendents of his father had a distinctive office and function which were very different to that given to the Levites as their helpers.

The Levites could not be priests even though the priests were "extracted" from the Tribe of Levi. Yet, the tithes collected from the Israelites were not for the priests as many assume, but were collected and kept by the Levites, the helpers of the priests. According to Numbers 18:21, 26-9, the tithes were given to them by God as their inheritance and reward for their services in the Sanctuary. When they collected the tithes, they in turn presented a tenth of it as the Lord's offering to the priests. In other words, Aaron's/priests' helpers received the tithes for themselves and paid a tithe of that tithe to the priests. The helpers received ninety percent (90%) of the tithe and ten percent (10%) went to the priests.

There were times when the Israelites refused to submit their tithes and offerings, and the priests and Levites had to work the soil to produce the needed food items for the survival of their families as was stated earlier. At some point in time, the Levites did not wait for the people to submit the tithes and offerings but descended on the productive fields to determine the amount and collect the tithes. Whether there was evidence that the people were not submitting the correct amount, or cheating, is not known, but I suspect that something of latter nature may have been in existence.

When Israel was taken captive and carried away into captivity, this brought an end to the sacrificial system until the day of their return and the restoration of the entire system. When in captivity, did the captives pay tithes on what they were given for their labor to sustain them? There is no biblical information or evidence to support answering the question in the positive or negative. What is known is that upon their liberation from captivity, the Sanctuary was restored and the system continued to function as before.

Over the years since the introduction of the tithing system in Israel, there appears to have been, at some point in time, a tremendous abundance of produce yielded by the land that in turn created an exponential increase in the tithe submitted to the Levites in the Temple. Storage and preservation became a serious problem that led to the constructional addition of a storehouse to the Temple. As a result of this, supervisors were appointed to administer the affairs of the storehouse contents. This Temple additional storehouse new idea is reflected in the passages of scripture found in 2Chronicles 31:11-12; Nehemiah 12:44; 13:4, 12 and Malachi 3:10.

In addition, there seems to have been an addition of a second and third tithe, and some confusion in reference to their application(s), but the word used for each one of these was the same used for the one that was designated for the Levites and priests, and this remains somewhat of a mystery. The tithing system remained as it was originally introduced for numerous years. It was organized as a reward for the work of the Levites primarily, and also for the priest in the Sanctuary. There was nothing originally attached to the giving of the tithe and offering as an incentive for the people to give. This was what God desired of His people and it was done without any expectation of a return. However, in the book of Malachi, it was introduced as an incentive to give with the expectation that God would open the windows of heaven and pour down bountiful blessings upon each individual who followed or was obedient to the tithing law.

Why was this notion introduced? I have no idea and no desire to speculate. It appears that the reason for giving was changed based on the introduction of this element. Instead of giving based on the Israelites' love for God and obedience to His tithing law for the support of His sacred work delivered by the Levites and priests in God's Temple, people were now looking to give in exchange for a generous return. This is the said concept that is preached and taught in twenty-first century churches that believe in and promote tithe paying.

193

If, however, there is an ulterior motive for giving, will the tithe be acceptable to God? If we are giving for the return of a blessing that is equal to or greater than that which was given, why not just keep what we have unless our perception of giving is tantamount to an investment. God wants us to give to His work of reconciliatory redemption out of a pure motive with no expectation of an earthly return. What else can we want in exchange for life, food, fresh air and the gift of grace, our Lord and Savior Jesus Christ, and the promise of life eternal with Him. These things are priceless and there is nothing we can give in exchange for them.

The other idea introduced in the same text in Malachi is that of becoming thieves or robbers of that which belongs to God, His tithe. The application of this idea may have been warranted and or appropriate in the Old Dispensation, but is it applicable in the New Dispensation? When Christ died on the cross, the entire sacrificial system, including tithing, was abrogated and there is no credible instructions, teachings or evidence in the New Testament that provide any contradiction to the abrogation of the entire system. Does this mean that a singular church, denomination or religion, is barred from the adoption of the tithing principle as the sole or partial means of financing its operations? I would think not once it is clearly understood that the chosen method is not a spiritual obligation but one that is voluntary. If one cannot participate, there is no robbery and guilt associated with one's "disobedience" to an annulled law since it is a voluntary practice in which one decides to or not to engage.

As was stated earlier, the death of Christ on the cross brought an end to the ceremonial laws, including the sacrificial, priestly and tithing, and triggered the renting of the Temple veil in two. This momentous sacrifice of the perfect Lamb of God, Jesus Christ, introduced a new "priestly system." Christ became our High Priest and all His disciples and or followers became his "priestly helpers." His death ushered in a High Priest, not after the Levitical/Aaronic type, but after that of Melchizedek who was neither genealogically connected to the Levites nor to Aaron.

This new order completely obliterated the types, shadows and symbols that the old sacrificial system represented, and replaced it with a new focus. No more animal sacrifices for sins, mediatory performances by priests since this was effectuated in Christ's sacrifice. The foci of the new order or new dispensation are preaching and teaching for the internal edification of the body of Christ in preparation for service, as well as baptism, communion etc.

With the introduction of this new order came the real "engine", the Holy Spirit, to power and make it a reality. Without the Spirit of God sent by the Father upon the request of Jesus, this new system would have been a total failure. It was the Spirit that fired up the disciples on the Day of Pentecost to get things rolling, and He continues to dwell with and in us for the same purpose in order to use us for the completion of the ministry of reconciliation.

We are, therefore, a Holy-Spirit driven people, all one and united in Christ with no hierarchical and office divisions since we are all equal and one in Jesus, and in the sight of God. We have been endowed with diverse gifts from the Spirit for the building up of the body of Christ to spiritual maturity in Him and for service. No one should even think that he/she is of greater importance to God due to his/her perception or misperception of the value placed on his/her role in or out the church. It is the Spirit of God who, if we allow Him, directs our total lives and we should be listening to hear His small voice as we make decisions in life.

The nature, function and scope of the new system are very different from the old and although directed by the Spirit of God, it appears to need an economic tool to sustain its operations or pay for the massive cost involved in taking the gospel into all the world. In the early church, as was mentioned previously, the foci were on evangelistic preaching and providing for the less fortunate or poor converts. The former is evidenced by the disciples' total involvement in preaching to the unsaved and not wanting to be distracted by the internal operations of the church. And the generosity of many new converts in selling their homes and lands, and donating the said money to care for the needs of the economically deprived, was a clear demonstration or example of the type of funding needed for the church's operation. Strangely enough, such generous contribution of funds to the church was at the exclusion of any fund for the so-called "clergy" and or evangelists, with some exception.

The critical question today is which method of funding for both the needs of the poor and the global dissemination of the gospel message is most appropriate from a biblical perspective? Is a voluntary tithing and offering system (one that does not produce the type of intended or unintended guilt before God in the body of Christ when the offering plates are passed around) sufficient to meet such massive goals? If such a funding system is insufficient for the realization of such a monumental need, should one of the above foci – preaching or the poor – be neglected in favor of the other? If so, which one should be given priority and what criterion or criteria should be applied to make such a determination?

It appears that such a choice has been made already as is so clearly seen in many Christian churches. Those that have reinstated the O.T. tithing law have earmarked it primarily for the salaries of their ministers/pastors whom they consider to be a type of priest (while failing to remember that all of God's children are priests) and at the total neglect of the poor. Or is it that the church should attempt to discover an equilibrium or more balanced system in which both foci are sufficiently financed for their effective realization?

The modern church needs to study very carefully how to balance financing the needs of the poor with that of the gospel dissemination. It cannot continue its financially imbalanced existence and hope to make genuine disciples for Jesus, people who will join the body of Christ and experience an operational model that is partly biblical. There may be a need to overhaul the entire system and reintroduce the principle of voluntarism for all those functioning in the local church (most of them still do) while only providing some economic assistance to those who are engaged in full-time evangelism. If not, the church will have to refocus its attention on rewarding all those who perform, if not minor roles, major roles in the local church if it decides to continue the unbiblical transference and application of the O.T. tithing principle to the Christian era.

It cannot be ignored that the disciples and particularly the elders of the early church were appointed by the Holy Spirit to be shepherds and overseers of the church (Acts. 20:28; 1Peter 5:2,3), and that they volunteered their time in order to ascertain fulfilling the needs of the poor and even though this was done on a more limited scale. It is also understandable that those who have been "selected" or chosen by the Spirit of God to preach or engage in full-time evangelism – preaching to and teaching the unsaved/un-churched – should be fully supported and not those who share the pulpits with the elders and others once per week. The latter is an exceptionally costly vocation especially when all the hidden costs are considered and this is at the exclusion of the other administrative and staff members at various levels of many church organizations.

As the early church's financial model is considered for modern application, no one should expect all church members to sell their lands and houses and give one hundred percent to the church and be classified as poor to claim assistance from the church or government. This would create an even greater burden on the church. The Holy Spirit should be allowed to continue His work amongst God's people and His voice should be listened to and applied in our giving. If the voice is not heard, members' decisions should be based on the New Testament new paradigmatic principle of giving on that which one has and not on what one does have.

Giving should not be based on any "legal" imposition that will surely place an external limit on members' benevolence, but on other principles such as love, a willing mind and a generous heart as one is impressed by the Spirit of God. Under such circumstances, there are some who will be able to give twenty, thirty, forty, fifty or even a greater percentage of their earnings and not be "legally" obligated to a ten percent limit. Let the Spirit of God work and let the church members respond in accordance with His influence.

I am convinced that the church needs much more money than it currently receives for the effectuation of its two foundational priorities: 1. Edification of the body of Christ for gospel proclamation, and 2. caring for the needs of the body members/the poor. When, therefore, an equilibrium of giving is created or achieved through the significant increases of those who can afford to give a greater percentage of their incomes to offset the smaller contributions and zero contribution of those who are economically deprived, and when the contributors are cognizant of how the funds are allocated/spent in reference to the two above-stated priority missions as a result of the implementation of an open-book policy, more than sufficient money will flow freely into the storehouse.

With the accomplishment of the significantly contributory increases of funds into the storehouse(s), there should be of necessity greater accountability of leaders by all members or their representatives and not by their higher-ups, "superiors" or colleagues in the organizations. This is critical due to the very naturally subtle influence of money temptation **("For the love of money is the root of all evil"** 1Timothy 6:10**)** and the deterioration of human nature over thousands of years since the fall of generic man. "Trust but verify" was the policy of the former President Ronald Reagan in his dealings with the former Soviet Union, and a noble and reasonable one to be applied to those in charged of the storehouse due to human susceptibility given the right circumstances.

The implementation of such a policy would assure God's people of the trustworthiness of their leaders if there are no discreditable situations that will call into question the credibility of leaders. It will also serve to protect the reputation of such leaders and provide even greater respect for those in charged of the storehouse finances.

It would be very difficult to close this book without reiterating the fact that when Christ died on the cross, the ceremonial laws including the priestly and tithing laws were completely annulled or made null and void. If this is not the case, then why is there neither any direct nor indirect instruction or recorded example of tithe paying in the New Testament by Jesus, His disciples, early church members or N.T. writers? Why is it that when one attempts to justify the current transference and application of the O.T. tithing law to the Christian era, there has to be so much theological extrapolation from the old dispensation to the new? Why are there so many hermeneutical errors made in the linking to and explanation of New Testament passages? Is it because there is no legitimate linkage?

This may be very difficult for many to accept due to the years of indoctrination on the significance of the tithing law in the New Dispensation and the consequences of being cursed by God for non-compliance which leads to the forfeiting of God's blessings and grace. If your conscience has been properly educated over the years and your conviction is unwaveringly firm that this is a law to which you must adhere, then follow your conscience based on both the assumed law and the following principle that *he that knoweth to do good and doeth it not, to him it is a sin* (James 4:17).

It must also be clearly stated, however, that all organizations, including the individual unconventional body of Christ or the church, have a right to determine the method(s) to be used in financing their operations. General Motors has a right to decide its own method of financing its operations. It is in the business of manufacturing and selling cars and trucks etc. and uses the profits to do so. If it goes out of business and the Red Cross purchases its building, a totally different operation in reference to its mission/purpose, philosophy and objectives will be instituted because of the nature of the Red Cross. It cannot utilize the same method of financing but must seek another because it depends on voluntary contributions for its operation.

In similar manner, the O.T. church was very different to that of the N.T. In a certain sense, the New Testament church's approach to its mission fulfillment is radically dissimilar to that of the O.T. The N.T. church is not required to sit and wait for the un-churched (unbelievers) to come and be instructed in the way of the Lord, but to go and preach/teach the gospel to all nations which will require a very different method of financing.

If religious entities decide to reinstate the tithing law as their most effective means of financing their churches' operations, they probably have that non-theological right, but not a God-given right to make their members feel guilty of violating an antiquated tithing law if some are not convinced that it is the biblically correct method prescribed in the New Testament for which Christians are required to adhere. If there is any divine revelation (and Christians must come to the realization that revelation has not closed or ceased because God is still revealing things to His people in this modern age and may have gifted us with this revelation) concerning the current existence and application of the tithing law/principle in the modern church, and its accuracy can be ascertained because it is in harmony with the Word of God, all should attempt to comprehend the exact message and comply with it.

To reiterate, however, any "new revelation" in reference to a proposal, explanation and or presentation that purports anything contrary to that presented in this book must be measured by information in Scripture or, it must be congruent with the teachings of the Bible on this subject matter. If specific instructions are given in the revelation as to how the tithe is to be distributed or used, any departure from it would be considered a contravention of the message and unworthy of church members' compliance. If the revelation does not harmonize with biblical/scriptural teachings, members should not be made to feel guilty if they are not convinced of its message. The Bible and the Bible alone is the sole rule of our faith (Solar Scriptura). No one should impose the O.T. tithing law on any Christian in the dispensation of grace due to the non-instructional evidence on tithing and the obsolescence of the entire sacrificial system, and all associated ceremonial laws at the death of Christ on the cross.

As was stated previously, there are about four categories of laws in the O.T. – the moral, civil, dietary and ceremonial. The moral, civil and dietary laws were not annulled at the cross. It was only the ceremonial laws that were abrogated when Christ died on that cross. Fortunately or unfortunately, the tithing law was a part of the ceremonial laws and came to an end with the death of Christ.

This is an idea which may be exceptionally difficult for many to accept, especially those who have been taught and or indoctrinated to believe that the tithing law was instituted prior the formation of Israel and the institution of the sacrificial system, and therefore, the rationale for its survival at the cross. As was stated earlier, the sacrifices were instituted relatively shortly after the Fall of generic man, and it did not survive the cross. So from a purely logical perspective, such a position or line of reasoning falls flat on its face.

If the author is theologically incorrect in his conclusion about the tithing law as being a component of the sacrificial/ceremonial law(s) that did not survive but was abrogated at the cross, I welcome an objective evaluation or critical analysis of this work in the form of a refutable articulation that will convince readers and me of any error. If this is humanly implausible, and some still believe that there is an error to correct but do not have the biblical proof on hand to refute it, do not make it a personal issue and turn up the ecclesiastical heat. Go back to the Word of God, our sole rule of faith, and conduct a more objectively thorough investigation to confirm or disconfirm your belief, or let go and let the Spirit of God work in due time to bring about the right conviction in the minds of Christians or church members.

In the long run, the Body of Christ, His church and family on earth may have to begin to rethink its position on this matter for a mindset and practice change, and eventual transformation of its structural components as a means of motivating more of God's people to voluntarily get involved in gospel proclamation. This will certainly reduce cost and speed up the realization of His mission, as we were instructed by Jesus, to take the gospel into all the world. God knows this is a necessity and that the church will not suffer financially as a result of the conclusive findings of and suggestion in this book. It, the Church of God, will triumphantly prosper by His grace and His grace only.

Bibliography

Baker, Warren, ed. The Complete Word Study Dictionary, Old Testament. Chattanooga, TN: AMG Publishers, 1994.

Barclay, William. The Gospel of Matthew, Vols. 1 & 2. Philadelphia: The Westminster Press, 1958.

Barclay, William. The Letters to the Corinthians. Philadelphia, PA: The Westminster Press, 1956.

Barclay, William. The Letter to the Hebrews. Philadelphia, PA: The Westminster Press, 1956.

Barnes, Albert. Barnes' Notes on the New Testament. Grand Rapids, MI: Kregel Publications, 1975.

Brown, Colin ed. The New International Dictionary of New Testament Theology. Grand Rapids, MI: Zondervan Publishing House, 1971.

Cole, Neil. Organic Leadership. Grand Rapids, MI: Baker Books, 2009

Edersheim, Alfred. The Life and Times of Jesus the Messiah. Grand rapids, MI: B.Edermans Publishing, Co., 1974.

Froom, LeRoy Edwin. Movement of Destiny. Washington, D.C.: Review and Herald Publishing Association, 1971.

Meyer's Commentary of the New Testament, Vol. 9 Peabody, MA: Hendricksen Publishing, Inc., 1984.

Pink, Authur W. An Exposition of Hebrews. Grand Rapids, MI: Baker book House, 1975.

The Expositor's Bible Commentary, Vol. 12. Grand Rapids, MI: The Zondervan Corporation, 1981.

Stott, John R. The Message of Ephesians. Downers Grove, Ill.: Inter-Varsity Press, 1986.

Seventh-day Adventists Believe: A Biblical Exposition of 27 Fundamental Doctrines. Washington, D.C.: Ministerial Association of General Conference of SDA, 1988.

Unger, Merrill F. Unger's Bible Dictionary. Chicago: Moody Press, 1975.

Zodhiates, Spiros, gen. ed. The Complete Word Study Dictionary. AMG Publishers, Chattanooga, TN, 1993.

CPSIA information can be obtained
at www.ICGtesting.com
Printed in the USA
LVOW10s0141250518

578413LV00016B/187/P